Oil Spills

by Don Nardo

LUCENT BOOKS
A part of Gale, Cengage Learning

GALE
CENGAGE Learning™

Detroit • New York • San Francisco • New Haven, Conn • Waterville, Maine • London

© 2011 Gale, Cengage Learning

LIBRARY OF CONGRESS CATALOGING-IN-PUBLICATION DATA

Nardo, Don, 1947-
  Oil spills / by Don Nardo.
    p. cm. -- (Hot topics)
  Includes bibliographical references and index.
  ISBN 978-1-4205-0624-2 (hardcover)
  1. Oil spills--Juvenile literature. I. Title.
  TD427.P4N36 2011
  363.738'2--dc22
                                                                    2011014601

Lucent Books
27500 Drake Rd.
Farmington Hills, MI 48331

ISBN-13: 978-1-4205-0624-2
ISBN-10: 1-4205-0624-2

Printed in the United States of America
1 2 3 4 5 6 7 15 14 13 12 11

Printed by Bang Printing, Brainerd, MN, 1st Ptg., 08/2011

CONTENTS

FOREWORD

Young people today are bombarded with information. Aside from traditional sources such as newspapers, television, and the radio, they are inundated with a nearly continuous stream of data from electronic media. They send and receive e-mails and instant messages, read and write online "blogs," participate in chat rooms and forums, and surf the Web for hours. This trend is likely to continue. As Patricia Senn Breivik, the former dean of university libraries at Wayne State University in Detroit, has stated, "Information overload will only increase in the future. By 2020, for example, the available body of information is expected to double every 73 days! How will these students find the information they need in this coming tidal wave of information?"

Ironically, this overabundance of information can actually impede efforts to understand complex issues. Whether the topic is abortion, the death penalty, gay rights, or obesity, the deluge of fact and opinion that floods the print and electronic media is overwhelming. The news media report the results of polls and studies that contradict one another. Cable news shows, talk radio programs, and newspaper editorials promote narrow viewpoints and omit facts that challenge their own political biases. The World Wide Web is an electronic minefield where legitimate scholars compete with the postings of ordinary citizens who may or may not be well-informed or capable of reasoned argument. At times, strongly worded testimonials and opinion pieces both in print and electronic media are presented as factual accounts.

Conflicting quotes and statistics can confuse even the most diligent researchers. A good example of this is the question of whether or not the death penalty deters crime. For instance, one study found that murders decreased by nearly one-third when the death penalty was reinstated in New York in 1995. Death penalty supporters cite this finding to support their argument that the existence of the death penalty deters criminals from committing murder. However, another study found that states without the death penalty have murder rates below the national average. This study is cited by opponents of capital punishment, who reject the claim that the death penalty deters murder. Students need context and clear, informed discussion if they are to think critically and make informed decisions.

The Hot Topics series is designed to help young people wade through the glut of fact, opinion, and rhetoric so that they can think critically about controversial issues. Only by reading and thinking critically will they be able to formulate a viewpoint that is not simply the parroted views of others. Each volume of the series focuses on one of today's most pressing social issues and provides a balanced overview of the topic. Carefully crafted narrative, fully documented primary and secondary source quotes, informative sidebars, and study questions all provide excellent starting points for research and discussion. Full-color photographs and charts enhance all volumes in the series. With its many useful features, the Hot Topics series is a valuable resource for young people struggling to understand the pressing issues of the modern era.

INTRODUCTION

A Serious Ongoing Threat

"On the night of April 20, 2010," former oil industry executive Bob Cavnar writes, "the oil and gas industry changed forever." Those dramatic words refer to one of the world's worst industrial accidents, which happened in the Gulf of Mexico about fifty miles southeast of Venice, Louisiana. The accident caused the largest ocean-based oil spill in history. Cavnar goes on to tell how the Deepwater Horizon oil-drilling platform, run by British Petroleum (BP), exploded in the gulf, allowing crude oil to begin gushing from the damaged wellhead below:

> Eleven good men lost their lives [as] the blast of the exploding deck engine set off a chain reaction of events that ignited the giant jet of oil and gas coming up through the drilling rig floor, incinerating everything nearby. . . . *Deepwater Horizon* had transformed into a latter-day *Titanic*. That night everything that could go wrong did go wrong. [The] oil began washing up on beaches and wetlands of Louisiana's fragile coastline weeks after the disaster, and giant subsurface plumes of it . . . reached close to the loop current that could take it beyond the Gulf of Mexico.[1]

For almost three months, the broken wellhead leaked oil as people across the world watched in disgust and horror. Cameras lowered to the sea floor from ships on the surface showed clear views of the oil bursting outward into gulf waters. Before the wellhead was finally capped in mid-July 2010, it had unleashed

When the Deepwater Horizon oil rig exploded on April 20, 2010, it became the largest ocean-based oil spill in history.

close to 5 million barrels, or 206 million gallons (780 million L), of crude oil. By that time, huge oil slicks had drifted northward to the coasts of Louisiana and neighboring states, fouling beaches and marshes and shutting down much of the local fishing industry.

Damages Wrought by Oil Spills

In many ways the disastrous effects of the 2010 BP oil spill, also referred to as the Gulf of Mexico oil spill, were illustrative of those of other large oil spills that occur around the globe on a fairly regular basis. Many of these mishaps take place in oceans, rivers, or other waterways. Others occur on land.

Wherever they happen, the long-term effects of these spills on the world's environment, and on human civilization as well, remain somewhat unclear. But nearly all of the scientists, government officials, and other experts who keep track of and study oil spills agree that the short-term effects are devastating. First, they point out, the local area affected by a spill suffers a wide range of environmental problems, from destruction of fragile wetlands to the killing of untold numbers of wildlife. According to the U.S. Environmental Protection Agency (EPA):

> Spilled oil poses serious threats to fresh water and marine [ocean] environments. It affects surface resources and a wide range of subsurface organisms that are linked in a complex food chain that includes human food resources. [The food chain is the natural system in which one species lives by eating one or more other species, which in turn subsist by consuming still others, and so forth.] Spilled oil can harm the environment in several ways, including the physical damages that directly impact wildlife and their habitats (such as coating birds or mammals with a layer of oil), and the toxicity of the oil itself, which can poison exposed organisms.[2]

A stunning example of a spill that created such negative environmental effects is that of the huge oil tanker *Exxon Valdez* (pronounced val-DEEZ). It ran aground on a reef in Alaska's Prince William Sound in March 1989. Some 240,000 barrels of crude oil, enough to fill the world's largest football stadium to the brim, escaped and smothered nearby coasts and ecosystems. (An ecosystem is a community of living things and the physical habitat, or environment, in which they live.) The *Exxon Valdez* oil spill adversely affected an astounding 1,300 miles (2,100 km) of coastline. Thousands of species of animals were assaulted, among them eagles, seagulls, and other birds; seals and otters; and whales, fish, and clams. Of the dozens of fish species affected, an estimated $12 million worth of herring alone were wiped out. Moreover, many of the harmful effects of the *Exxon Valdez* accident lasted for more than two decades. Others are expected to continue ravaging the area for another decade or more.

The human costs of large oil spills are also often high. Cleanup crews are exposed to toxic materials and fumes, for example. Such exposure has caused numerous documented cases of sickness, including recurring nausea, nervous system damage, and irritation of the respiratory system. There have also been a number of mental health concerns. A research project sponsored by the University of New Hampshire and the National Oceanic and Atmospheric Administration (NOAA) reported in 2010:

> Oil spills and spill responses can cause high levels of stress and psychological trauma, including post-traumatic stress. The economic impacts on livelihood and family aspirations, anxieties associated with exposure to toxic chemicals, the stress of engaging in a large scale court battle, and the loss of valued landscape and ecological systems all contribute to stress on coastal residents and cleanup workers.[3]

Another important aspect of the damage done to humans by big oil spills is economic in nature. When spills contaminate the sea, fishing industry workers and others who make their livings from ocean-related industries suffer from short- or long-term unemployment. Local businesses on land are also adversely affected, especially restaurants that sell seafood, companies that clean and package fish and clams, and other seafood-based businesses. In some cases tourism suffers as well. The 2010 BP oil spill, for instance, caused a marked reduction in tourism along the coasts of Louisiana and other gulf states. According to the U.S. Travel Association, between 2010 and 2013 the oil leaked by the Deepwater Horizon wellhead is expected to cause a loss of about $23 billion in tourism-related industries, which normally generate some $34 billion per year in the area.

Being Proactive

If large-scale oil spills were rare occurrences, they would be of little concern when looking at the global picture. However, the world, particularly its increasing numbers of industrialized nations, uses enormous amounts of oil each year. Indeed, human civilization used an estimated 85 million barrels each day in 2010—a total of roughly 31 billion barrels for that year.

The oil industry tries to drill, refine, and ship all this oil in a safe manner. Over time, however, human error, natural disasters, and terrorism have taken a terrible toll in spilled oil. For example, in December 1976 a tanker ship called the *Argo Merchant* ran aground off the island of Nantucket (in southern Massachusetts) causing about 183,000 barrels of oil to spill and create an oil slick 100 miles (160 km) long. In January 1993, four years after the *Exxon Valdez* unleashed ruinous plumes in Alaska, heavy seas caused a major accidental oil spill along the coasts of northern Scotland's Shetland Islands. Approximately 549,000 barrels spewed from the damaged tanker ship. Almost exactly five years later, in January 1998, a ruptured oil pipeline in the African nation of Nigeria dumped 40,000 barrels of oil into the local environment.

More big spills followed. To name only a few, in excess of 14,000 barrels of oil poured from a barge into Brazil's Amazon rain forest in February 2000. In November 2004 a tanker let loose more than 13,000 barrels of crude oil into the Delaware River between Philadelphia and southern New Jersey. Three years later, in December 2007, a spill off the coast of South Korea introduced more than 700,000 barrels of slimy, toxic oil into the surrounding environment.

As bad as these disasters were, they were dwarfed by the 2010 BP oil spill. This indicates that such incidents remain a serious ongoing threat to the global environment and human society. The day may well come when humanity finds safer kinds of energy to power its civilization. But experts predict that that day lies at least a few decades in the future and very possibly longer.

Until then, they say, the best tool that can be wielded to minimize the number of major spills and their detrimental effects is knowledge. Continued studies of the causes, impacts, cleanup methods, and potential preventative measures of oil spills will allow scientists, oil companies, and government agencies to more effectively learn from past mistakes. One prominent group of researchers explains it this way:

> Experience with oil spills inside and outside the United States demonstrates that oil spills produce dramatic consequences for people's lives. To better prepare for responding to spills, it is wise to learn from experience and be proactive about planning for how to deal with impacts to humans. Hopefully, a broad understanding of the human dimensions of oil spill hazards can help these responders make wise decisions.[4]

WHY THE WORLD USES SO MUCH OIL

A frequent theme of modern television and radio broadcasts and newspaper and magazine articles is modern civilization's dependence on oil, or petroleum. Sheryl Joaquin, an expert on petroleum products and their uses, defines this crucial substance as

> a naturally occurring hydrocarbon-based liquid which is sometimes present in porous rocks beneath the earth's surface. Petroleum is formed by the slow alteration of organic [living] remains over time. It consists of a mixture of liquid hydrocarbon compounds [chains or rings of carbons atoms surrounded by hydrogen atoms] and varies widely in composition, color, [and] density.[5]

Often humanity's dependence on oil is described in negative terms. This is partly because large-scale oil spills happen across the world many times in each succeeding decade. These disasters often ravage the environment and cost billions of dollars to clean up. Many people feel that if humanity could largely replace petroleum with cleaner sources of energy (such as solar, wind, and geothermal), such spills would become rare. On this point there is little or no debate among experts.

In addition, dependence on oil is frequently seen in a negative light because of claims by scientists and other expert observers that sooner or later oil supplies will run out. That claim is still debated, often hotly. However, such claims and debates remain separate from and mostly irrelevant to the issue of oil dependence. No matter how much oil still exists for humanity to exploit, experts are virtually unanimous in saying that modern society is dependent on oil. As geologist Jeremy Leggett

Many products other than fuels are made from crude oil, including plastics, medicines, fabrics, and many household items.

puts it, "We have allowed oil to become vital to virtually everything we do."[6] It therefore follows that as long as people continue to use enormous amounts of oil, from time to time some of it will spill, causing environmental and economic damage.

The dependence to which Leggett and other scientists refer is based partly on the fact that petroleum provides a major portion of the energy and fuels used by modern civilization. For example, more than 40 percent of the energy used in the United States each year comes from oil. Moreover, about 97 percent of the country's transportation fuels are produced from crude oil.

Yet humanity's oil dependence is not based solely on the use of petroleum for gasoline and other fuels. In fact, oil is also used in a wide array of everyday products. These include huge numbers of household items, medicines, fabrics, plastics, and other manufactured goods. "Thousands of petroleum products are used and taken for granted each day by people all over the world,"[7] researcher Anna Wegis points out.

Ancient Uses of Petroleum

Many people are surprised to find out that this widespread use of petroleum for numerous industrial and everyday needs is not strictly a modern phenomenon. Indeed, far from new, it began in a limited way in ancient times and over the centuries became more common and extensive.

Oil Consumption Around the World – 2009

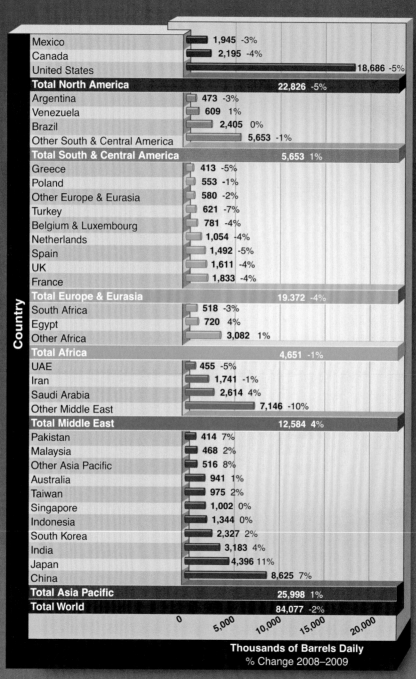

Country	Thousands of Barrels Daily	% Change 2008–2009
Mexico	1,945	-3%
Canada	2,195	-4%
United States	18,686	-5%
Total North America	**22,826**	**-5%**
Argentina	473	-3%
Venezuela	609	1%
Brazil	2,405	0%
Other South & Central America	5,653	-1%
Total South & Central America	**5,653**	**1%**
Greece	413	-5%
Poland	553	-1%
Other Europe & Eurasia	580	-2%
Turkey	621	-7%
Belgium & Luxembourg	781	-4%
Netherlands	1,054	-4%
Spain	1,492	-5%
UK	1,611	-4%
France	1,833	-4%
Total Europe & Eurasia	**19.372**	**-4%**
South Africa	518	-3%
Egypt	720	4%
Other Africa	3,082	1%
Total Africa	**4,651**	**-1%**
UAE	455	-5%
Iran	1,741	-1%
Saudi Arabia	2,614	4%
Other Middle East	7,146	-10%
Total Middle East	**12,584**	**4%**
Pakistan	414	7%
Malaysia	468	2%
Other Asia Pacific	516	8%
Australia	941	1%
Taiwan	975	2%
Singapore	1,002	0%
Indonesia	1,344	0%
South Korea	2,327	2%
India	3,183	4%
Japan	4,396	11%
China	8,625	7%
Total Asia Pacific	**25,998**	**1%**
Total World	**84,077**	**-2%**

Thousands of Barrels Daily
% Change 2008–2009

Taken from: British Petroleum/Statistical Review of World Energy.
www.guardian.co.uk/news/datablog/2010/Jun/09bp-energy-statistics-consumption-reserves-energy.

While no large-scale oil industry existed in the ancient world, small quantities of petroleum did occasionally rise to the surface in various places, especially in the Middle East, where large subsurface deposits of oil exist. Puddles of crude oil also frequently appeared in India, Egypt, and southern Europe.

Finding such petroleum pools, people tended to use the slippery substance in some of the same ways they used a number of plant and animal oils. Olive oil, for example, was commonly used to fuel oil lamps, as a lubricant, and as a base for medicines and perfumes. In the late first century A.D., Roman naturalist Pliny the Elder described deposits of crude oil, which he called bitumen, in Palestine, Syria, Mesopotamia (what is now Iraq), and the Italian island of Sicily. In the latter, he said, the inhabitants used bitumen in place of olive oil in lamps. They also rubbed it on donkeys and other pack animals to heal skin irritations and ailments.

The petroleum deposits Pliny mentioned in Mesopotamia, specifically those near the major city of Babylon, were also described earlier by the fifth-century B.C. Greek historian Herodotus. In his *Histories*, the first known conventional history book, the so-called father of history tells about his journey to Mesopotamia, then ruled by the Persians. Not far from Babylon, he says, near the town of Ardericca, was a pit containing salt and two oily substances. He calls one bitumen and the other oil, probably making a distinction between a partially solidified form and a liquid form of petroleum:

> They [the locals] draw [up] the liquid with a swipe [a long pole balanced horizontally on a pivot]. Instead of a bucket, half a wineskin is attached to the rope at one end, and they dip with this, draw up the stuff, and pour it into a [pottery] tank. From the tank it is drained off into another receptacle. . . . The Persian word for oil is *rhadinace*. It is very dark in color and has a strong smell.[8]

The bitumen and oil collected in this manner had uses similar to those described by Pliny. The Persians, evidently like the Babylonians before them, also employed the bitumen as a kind of mortar for construction projects. Herodotus comments on its

Pliny the Elder on Bitumen

The first-century A.D. Roman scholar Pliny the Elder says the following about how people in his day use the diverse oil products, which he calls bitumen, found in natural seeps.

> Bitumen has similar properties to sulfur. In some places it resembles mud, in others a mineral. It issues with the consistency of mud from the Dead Sea [in Palestine], and is found as a mineral in Syria. . . . There is, however, a liquid form of bitumen, such as that from [Mesopotamia]. There is also a white variety in Babylon. . . . There is also a bitumen of the consistency of [olive] oil. It is found in a spring at Agrigentum in Sicily and pollutes the spring's waters. The inhabitants collect it on bunches of reeds to which it quickly adheres, and use it instead of lamp-oil [i.e., instead of olive oil] and also as a cure for scab in beasts of burden.

Pliny the Elder. *Natural History.* Excerpted in *Pliny the Elder: Natural History; A Selection.* Translated by John H. Healy. New York: Penguin, 1991, pp. 339–340.

use in Babylon's long and high defensive walls, saying, "While the digging [of the moat] was going on, the earth that was shoveled out was formed into bricks, which were baked in ovens as soon as a sufficient number were made. Then, using hot bitumen for mortar, the workmen began . . . to erect [the] wall."[9]

Medieval Extraction and Uses

The ancient method of extracting petroleum products, as described by Herodotus, was small-scale, crude, and time consuming. Perhaps if faster, larger-scale methods had been known, oil might have been used on a much wider scale. The first culture to develop a large-scale drilling method was that of the early medieval Chinese. Beginning in about A.D. 300 and continuing into the 900s, they used a sophisticated extraction process from wells dug as deep as 850 feet (259 m). At first this technique was used to mine salt brine and natural gas (mainly methane). But over the centuries the Chinese and other Asian societies adapted the same drilling process for the extraction of petroleum. Scholars Peter James and Nick Thorpe describe this slow but ingenious process:

> At the top of the borehole, a shaft was dug with spades until hard rock was reached. The shaft was then filled with carefully prepared stones, pierced with holes in the middle, stacked one on top of the other up to ground level, and perfectly centered so that a long hole, eight to fourteen inches in diameter, extended down through them to the rock. Then the drilling began, using a drill with a cast-iron bit suspended from a derrick by bamboo cables. The bit was lifted by a man jumping onto a lever and came crashing down when he leaped off again. Through this laborious process, one to three feet a day could be drilled. When the brine was reached, it was collected in a bamboo tube with a valve at the bottom and hoisted to the surface.[10]

From as early as A.D. 850, the Chinese, along with Muslims living along the western shores of the Caspian Sea, obtained liquid petroleum this way. Evidence shows that they used much of it for their lamps, in place of animal and plant oils. For instance, in about 1250 the Venetian merchant Marco Polo visited what is now the nation of Georgia, lying between the Caspian and Black Seas. In his now classic book recounting his travels, he writes,

> Near the Georgian border, there is a spring from which gushes a stream of oil [that is drilled] in such abundance that [it can fill] a hundred ships. . . . This oil is not good to eat [like olive oil or oil derived from animal fat], but it is good for burning and as a salve for men and camels affected with itch or scab. Men come from a long distance to fetch this oil, and in all the neighborhood [region] no other oil is burned but this.[11]

Oil in Early America

None of the ancient and medieval sources that mention petroleum say anything about oil spills. In all likelihood, that is because oil was still used on a relatively small scale, and whatever spillage occurred was tiny and not seen as worth writing about. The first country to develop a large-scale petroleum industry in which spills would eventually become newsworthy was the early United States.

U.S. oil deposits were first found and exploited in western Pennsylvania, several miles north of Pittsburgh. In about 1755 colonial Americans gave the name "Oil Creek" to the area, which for roughly three centuries had been inhabited by a Native American people, the Seneca. Even before the Seneca arrived on the scene (sometime in the 1400s or 1500s), earlier Native Americans, often referred to as Paleo-Indians, as well as Mound Builders, had visited the Oil Creek region. They found small pools or streams of oil gurgling from the ground there. Desiring to use the dark liquid in their religious rituals, they dug narrow trenches, which allowed more of it to reach the surface. When the first whites reached Oil Creek centuries later, some of these trenches were still visible.

OIL PRODUCTION IN DECLINE?

"Scientists [warn] that the end of oil is coming sooner than governments and oil companies are prepared to admit. . . . Scientists led by the London-based Oil Depletion Analysis Centre, say that global production of oil is set to peak in [2011] before entering a steepening decline which will have massive consequences for the world economy and the way that we live our lives."—Daniel Howden, foreign editor of the UK newspaper the *Independent*.

Daniel Howden. "World Oil Supplies Are Set to Run Out Faster than Expected, Warn Scientists." *Independent* (London), June 14, 2007. www.independent.co.uk/news/science/world-oil-supplies-are-set-to-run-out-faster-than-expected-warn-scientists-453068.html.

The petroleum at Oil Creek was also valuable to the Seneca and colonial whites. According to Pennsylvania State University scholar Brian Black, the Seneca "skimmed the oil from the water's surface, using a blanket as a sponge or dipping a container into the water, and then used the collected crude oil as an ointment or skin coloring."[12] The whites also used the local oil as an ointment to make aching joints feel better. All of these uses of the oil in the area were small-scale.

The Oil Creek, Pennsylvania, area was used by Native Americans long before colonial times. By 1864 it had become the first major oil-producing field in the United States.

A few decades after Pennsylvania, including Oil Creek, became part of the United States, a businessman named Samuel Kier sought a way to more extensively exploit the local petroleum. In 1849 he bottled and marketed it under the name "Rock Oil," and later "Seneca Oil," as a general remedy for minor illness. Kier's medicine business was largely unsuccessful, however. So he started looking for other ways to exploit the oil and soon discovered, as some of the ancients had, that it could be used as a fuel for lamps. He refined, or processed, the oil to make kerosene, which burned even better. In fact, in 1853 Kier opened the country's first oil refinery in Pittsburgh to produce his fuel, which he called "Carbon Oil."

Although Kier's refinery did well, he was not as successful as he might have been. This was partly because he had no patent, or set of exclusive rights granted by the government, for making fuel from petroleum. Also, he continued to extract the oil by digging with shovels and skimming it into a barrel, much as the Seneca had.

Other entrepreneurs (enterprising businesspersons) quickly took advantage of Kier's lack of vision. Chief among them was a young New Hampshire man named George Bissell. He conceived the idea of drilling for the petroleum, which he hoped would produce much larger quantities of the substance than digging for and skimming it. The idea was to use drilling techniques that had long been used for extracting salt (very much like those employed by the medieval Chinese).

To put his plan into action, Bissell first found some financial backers, including Connecticut banker James Townsend, and in 1854 established the Pennsylvania Rock Oil Company. A key early figure in the operation was former railroad worker Edwin Drake, who did the actual drilling. In 1857 Bissell's company sent Drake to Titusville, in Pennsylvania's Oil Creek region. Environmental expert Laura De Angelo tells how what many at the time viewed as a reckless venture ended up paying off in a big way:

> The operation was initially a grand failure and adopted the moniker [nickname] "Drake's Folly" from the locals who thought Drake a fool for his ventures. This perception, however . . . changed alongside the growing success of the drilling operation. Upon Drake's first drilling success in Titusville on August 27, 1859, the well produced 25 barrels of oil from a depth of only 69.5 feet. This discovery, although seemingly unimpressive by today's standards, would soon grab the attention of the nation. A plan that had initially been viewed as preposterous and empty of promise had indeed proven successful. This realization [created a] frenzy and a boom of development often compared to the California Gold Rush. The Pennsylvania oil industry flourished and the state [soon] became the provider of one-half of the world's oil.[13]

Thereafter, the expansion of oil production in the United States was rapid. In 1860, only a year after Drake's initial success,

American drillers brought up some 500,000 barrels of the dark crude. Two years later that figure increased to 3 million barrels, and by 1880 more than 26 million barrels were pumped annually. One of the major milestones in that period was the establishment of the Standard Oil Company by entrepreneur John D. Rockefeller Sr. (born 1839) and some associates. Standard Oil bought up a majority of the existing oil refineries (which turned the crude oil into gasoline and other products), in that way cornering the market. But that market had only begun to grow. In the 1880s large oil deposits were found in Ohio, followed by

In 1857 Edwin Drake, left foreground, stands in front of "Drake's Folly," America's first oil well, in Titusville, Pennsylvania.

discoveries of major oil fields in California, Texas, and Oklahoma in the 1890s. Not long after that, an enormous new market for petroleum—gasoline for early automobiles—emerged, and in the year 1920 U.S. drillers produced the then incredible amount of 440 million barrels of oil. (In the meantime, in 1911 Standard Oil broke up, creating the companies that later became the oil giants Exxon, Sohio, Mobil, Chevron, Amoco, and Conoco.)

Crucial to Everyday Life

Although the United States long led the way in oil production, other parts of the world eventually caught up. Canada, Russia, and especially Saudi Arabia and several other Middle Eastern nations demonstrated that they possessed huge oil reserves, too. As a result, by 2010 world petroleum production had risen to 85 million barrels a day. That is equivalent to 31 billion barrels per year. Moreover, considering that a standard barrel contains 42 gallons (159 L), global oil production came to roughly 1.3 trillion gallons (5 trillion L) in 2010.

ALTERNATIVE ENERGIES ON THE RISE

"The world is not running out of oil anytime soon. A gradual transitioning on the global scale away from a fossil-based energy systems may in fact happen during the 21st century. The root causes, however, will most likely have less to do with lack of supplies and far more with superior alternatives."—Nansen G. Saleri, president of Quantum Reservoir Impact in Houston, Texas.

Nansen G. Saleri. "The World Has Plenty of Oil." *Peak Oil News*, March 4, 2008. http://peakoil.blogspot.com/2008/03/world-has-plenty-of-oil.html.

Worthy of note is that as the amount of oil pumped over the course of the last century and a half increased, so did the number of ways that human civilization used the oil. In Standard Oil's great moment in the sun in the late 1800s and early 1900s, most petroleum was used for making gasoline for cars

Where Did Oil Come From?

The often-asked question of how oil came to be in the first place is concisely answered here by Gisele Fong, an expert on oil and its uses.

The youngest barrel of oil is one million years old; a typical barrel is 40 million years older than that. In spite of the nickname "dino juice," oil doesn't come from dead dinosaurs, but rather from tiny, one-celled aquatic plants and animals that take light from the sun and convert it into energy. 600–300 million years ago a series of specific geological events began in the ancient oceans, lakes, and swamps of the world that eventually created crude oil. . . . The ancient oceans were full of microscopic life. As these organisms died—especially plankton, diatoms, foraminifera, and radiolarian—they sank to the sand and mud on the ocean floor where the organic material mixed with sediments to form (over thousands of years) a fine-grained shale or source rock. As new layers were deposited on top of the source rock, the heat and pressure they exerted distilled the organic material in the source rock, turning it into natural crude oil. . . . If any one of these events had failed to occur, oil would never have formed. . . . Although oil is still forming, it is not renewable, as we are using it far faster than it is being created.

Gisele Fong et al. "What Is Oil?" www.endoil.org/site/ c.ddJGKNNnFmG/b.4051695/k.938D/What_is_Oil .htm.

and kerosene for lighting. However, science and industry steadily found many more uses for oil, a few of which a modern environmental researcher lists here:

If you have touched a chain on a bicycle, you have touched some oil. The black stuff that appears on your fingers is an oil that makes the chains on your bike run smoothly. We use oil to make asphalt which can help us pave our roads. You can get examples of oil at a toy store, a hardware store, or a drugstore, because oil is made into plastics, which could be any of your toys or CD players. Oil is also used in medicines, ink, paints, and to create some electricity.[14]

Oil producers pumped 1.3 trillion gallons of oil out of the world's oil fields in 2010.

Some other common uses of and products made from petroleum include: so-called bunker fuel, or "heavy oil," for powering large ships; synthetic (artificial, or human-made) rubber for car and truck tires and rubber soles on the bottoms of shoes; synthetic fibers, among them polyester, nylon, and acrylic for making clothes, curtains, and carpets; fertilizers to make plants grow bigger and healthier and pesticides to keep insects and other pests from eating those plants; paints and paint additives; detergents for washing clothes and dishes; photographic film; food additives that help make canned food last longer on grocery store shelves; medicines, including some pain relievers; makeup for both theatrical and everyday uses; perfumes, combs, and shampoo; candle wax; hair dyes and hair spray; fishing rods, golf balls, and beach umbrellas; and many more.

This list of modern uses for petroleum proves Leggett's point that humanity has allowed that substance to become an absolutely crucial component of everyday life. In fact, he says, modern industrialized societies are downright dependent on oil. Leggett sums up the situation this way:

Ninety per cent of all our transportation, whether by land, air or sea, is fuelled by oil. Ninety-five per cent of all goods in shops involve the use of oil. Ninety-five per cent of all our food products require oil use. Just to farm a single cow and deliver it to market requires six barrels of oil, enough to drive a car from New York to Los Angeles. The [amount of oil the] world consumes . . . is rising fast, as it has done for decades. The almost universal expectation is that it will keep doing so for years to come.[15]

Oil Spills Inevitable

Leggett and other experts add that part of what makes this oil dependency problematic is that pumping, containing, storing, and transporting the oil are not perfect sciences. So spills are bound to occur on a periodic basis. Underscoring this fact, in 1989, following a major oil spill, top officials at the EPA gave U.S. president George H.W. Bush this sober assessment:

Some oil spills may be inevitable. Oil is a vital resource that is inherently dangerous to use and transport. We therefore must balance environmental risks with the nation's energy requirements. The nation must recognize that there is no fail-safe prevention, preparedness, or response system. Technology and human organization can reduce the chance of accidents and mitigate [lessen the impact of] their effects, but may not stop them from happening.[16]

CHAPTER 2

THE CAUSES OF
OIL SPILLS

When offshore drilling rigs like the Deepwater Horizon and huge tanker ships like the *Argo Merchant* and *Exxon Valdez* produce accidental oil spills, they make headlines around the globe. News reports leave large numbers of people aghast at the environmental destruction. Worries about the economic costs of such disasters also spread far and wide.

Some oil spills are intentional—some oil companies secretly dump oil sludge into the environment.

World's Biggest Oil Spills

IN MILLIONS OF GALLONS

	Location	Year	Cause	
1.	Persian Gulf	1991	Intentional*	240
2.	Gulf of Mexico	2010	Blowout	210
3.	Gulf of Mexico	1979	Well blowout	140
4.	Trinidad	1979	Ship collision	84.2
5.	Persian Gulf	1983	Blowout	80
6.	Uzbekistan	1992	Blowout	80
7.	South Africa	1983	Tanker fire	78.5
8.	Portsall, France	1978	Ship grounding	68.7
9.	North Atlantic	1988	Tanker rupture	43.1
10.	Libya	1980	Blowout	42
11.	Land's End, Britain	1967	Tanker rupture	38.2

*Intentional release by Iraq

SOURCE: Oil Spill Intelligence Report

Because of all that publicity and the distress that accompanies it, many people assume that most oil spills derive from ocean-based tanker and drilling rig accidents. However, petroleum gets into the environment in numerous other ways, some of them surprising to casual observers. Some of these incidents occur on land, for example. Many result from equipment failure or human error in refineries or storage facilities, while others happen when tanker trucks are involved in highway accidents. Still other oil spills are intentional. Companies have secretly dumped oil sludge to save money, for instance, and in wartime one side has purposely destroyed either the enemy's or its own oil wells to create chaos. Also among the leading causes of oil leaking into the environment are simple inefficiency and carelessness. According to commentator S.E. Smith,

Numerous land-based engines such as those used to run cars function on petroleum fuel and use petroleum-based lubricants. [Because they do not burn with 100 percent efficiency, small amounts] of these substances are slowly released, accumulating on roads and in the ground and ultimately ending up in the ocean. The problem is compounded by people who do not dispose of things like used motor oil safely. Dumping used motor oil in the drain is illegal in many places because many drains run directly to the sea.[17]

Natural Causes of Oil Spills

All of the causes of oil spills mentioned so far involve human or mechanical error or people's deliberate releases of oil. Though these sources of oil leakage into the environment are significant, nature itself is often a culprit in the process. Earthquakes sometimes cause oil pipelines and storage tanks to rupture, for example. Heavy fog, hurricanes, and even large thunderstorms have also brought about major oil spill disasters.

One of the worst examples of weather-related calamities of this sort took place in 1979. Two large oil tankers, the *Atlantic Empress* and *Aegean Captain*, were cruising the waters near the island of Tobago, north of Venezuela. On July 19 a huge storm suddenly engulfed the area. Enormous waves and blinding sheets of rain pummeled the vessels, causing them to lose their bearings. Eventually, the crews of the ships made visual contact. But it was too late, and they collided violently. Moreover, this disaster was soon followed by an unexpected and awful aftermath, as oil industry security consultant Auke Visser describes:

> The *Atlantic Empress* had 275,000 tons of oil aboard; the *Aegean Captain* was carrying 200,000 tons. After the collision, fires broke out all over the *Atlantic Empress* and on the bow of the *Aegean Captain*. The *Aegean* managed to control the fire and then was towed toward Trinidad. Some oil was spilled during the towing, but a fair portion of the cargo was transferred successfully to other vessels. The *Atlantic Empress*, however, had more difficulties.

While it was still burning, it was towed toward the open sea. Oil continued to leak, burning on top of the ocean waters. Four days after the collision, with the fire still out of control, an explosion rocked the ship. There was another explosion the next day. Still, efforts to stop the fire and prevent more oil from spilling into the ocean continued. On July 29, 10 days after the fire began, another powerful explosion ended hopes of containing the blaze. On August 3, the *Atlantic Empress* sunk to the ocean bottom, leaving only a burning oil slick behind.[18]

Because the *Atlantic Empress* sank in deep water, very little oil made it to nearby beaches. However, the toll on wildlife in the ocean was apparently large. Expert observers estimated that millions of fish and other creatures in the area died from exposure to the leaked oil.

LIFE IS ABOUT TRADE-OFFS

"We can't have all good things and no bad things. In life as it actually exists, we must choose and make trade-offs. BP appears to have been negligent in its management of sinking the well. . . . The situation is tragic. Yet it is not one that anybody wanted. It is a terrible contingency in an unavoidably risky world." —Robert Higgs, senior fellow at The Independent Institute.

Robert Higgs. "Disaster, Heartbreak, and Unavoidable Trade-Offs." Independent Institute, June 30, 2010. www.independent.org/blog/index.php?p=6806.

Another way that nature unleashes petroleum into the environment, both on land and in the sea, is through what scientists call natural seepages, or seeps. According to NOAA:

Apart from oil spills caused by human actions, oil also is released into the environment from natural oil seeps in the ocean bottom. One of the best-known areas where this happens is Coal Oil Point along the California Coast near Santa Barbara. An estimated 2,000 to 3,000 gallons of crude oil is released naturally from the ocean bottom every day just a few miles offshore from this beach.[19]

Such areas containing natural oil seepages have been known for a long time in various other parts of the world. For instance, a seep in Israel's Dead Sea was well known as far back as biblical times. On the other side of the globe, when Christopher Columbus landed on the island of Trinidad during his third voyage in 1498, he found a large oil seep. His crew used some

Oil seepage is burned off in Indonesia. Experts are unsure of how much oil enters the environment through natural seepage, but it may be more than what is accidentally spilled.

The Biggest Oil Consumers

According to the *World Fact Book*, compiled annually by the U.S. Central Intelligence Agency (CIA), in 2010 the world's fifteen largest consumers of oil were:

Country	Barrels of Oil per Day
United States	19,500,000
European Union	14,390,000
China	7,999,000
Japan	4,785,000
Russia	2,800,000
India	2,670,000
Germany	2,569,000
Brazil	2,520,000
Saudi Arabia	2,380,000
Canada	2,260,000
South Korea	2,175,000
France	1,986,000
Mexico	1,772,000
United Kingdom	1,710,000
Italy	1,639,000

CIA. "Oil Consumption." *World Fact Book*. www.nationsencyclopedia.com/WorldStats/CIA-World-Factbook-Oil-consumption.html.

of the bitumen they found in the seep to waterproof the hulls of their ship. Over time, the Trinidad oil pit became known as Asphalt Lake. In the 1800s it became the source of tens of millions of tons of oily tars that were used for more than a century to pave roads in the United States and Canada. The surface deposits of petroleum exploited for centuries at Oil Creek, in Pennsylvania, are another example of a natural seepage of oil. Still another is La Brea Tar Pits, in Los Angeles, California, where many prehistoric animals got caught and met their ends in the semisolid petroleum. (Scientists found the remains of several of these beasts during the twentieth century.)

Experts are unsure of just how much oil enters the environment from natural seepages across the world. Some think that the amount may well be larger than the quantity spilled as a result of human activities. As for what happens to all that oil released from seeps, studies show that some solidifies either on land or the ocean bottom. An unknown quantity is eaten by bacteria. Most of the rest disperses into the seas, where its impact depends on how many plants and animals happen to make contact with it. Most scientists deem it normal, or part of the natural order, for a certain number of living things to be killed this way in a given decade or century.

Accidental Tanker Spills

Oil spills caused by human activities are not part of the natural order, however. Among the most famous of these incidents are those involving tanker ships, mainly because the disasters are so dramatic and the amount of oil they unleash into the environment is so large. Many oil tanker mishaps result from the failure of faulty or aging equipment and/or human error. Another related cause is equipment design or routine procedures that unexpectedly pose unnecessary dangers to tankers.

The latter factor appears to have brought about one of the more spectacular tanker accidents on record—that of the Liberian vessel *Sansinena*, on December 17, 1976. The 810-foot (247m) ship was docked in Los Angeles Harbor at the time. Investigators later concluded that flammable vapors from the oil cargo rose up and mixed with oxygen in the air. At the time, leaving some of the cargo area open to the air was routine practice for many tankers, in part because it was assumed that the fumes would continue to dissipate into the air circulating through the harbor and nearby city. This time, however, the vapors built up onboard to dangerous levels, a development that went undetected. Eventually, an ignition source that remains unidentified—perhaps someone lighting a match—came into contact with the vapor. This touched off an enormous explosion that tore the vessel to shreds. In the words of a spokesperson for NOAA,

> The force of the explosion propelled the main deck over the cargo tanks into the air. When the deck landed, it severed a 36-inch cargo line on top of the inshore isolation valve. This severed line fed fuel to the fire until response personnel discovered and capped it on December 21. Nine lives were lost as a result of the explosion. Debris and oil scattered in all directions. Approximately 400 boats in the vicinity were damaged by the fine mist of airborne oil, resulting in millions of dollars

The tanker Exxon Valdez *sits grounded on a reef in April 1989. The tanker spilled forty thousand barrels of oil into the ocean.*

in property damage. An estimated 30,000 barrels of oil were released into Los Angeles Harbor from the ship and the severed pipeline. A U.S. Coast Guard boat and a Los Angeles City Fire Department boat arrived on-scene within five minutes of the explosion to assist in fire-fighting and rescue operations. Pollution surveys were conducted after the fire was under control. Initial reports concluded that much of the oil had burned off, but on December 19, underwater divers discovered a large quantity of oil on the bottom of the harbor.[20]

The *Amoco Cadiz* Disaster

The International Tanker Owners Pollution Federation Limited (ITOPF) provides this concise overview of the famous *Amoco Cadiz* oil spill.

The tanker *Amoco Cadiz* ran aground off the coast of Brittany [in northwestern France] on 16 March 1978, following a steering gear failure. Over a period of two weeks the entire cargo of 223,000 tonnes [metric tons] of light Iranian and Arabian crude oil and 4,000 tonnes of bunker fuel was released into heavy seas. Much of the oil quickly formed a viscous water-in-oil emulsion, increasing the volume of pollutant by up to five times. By the end of April oil and emulsion had contaminated 320km of the Brittany coastline, and had extended as far east as the Channel Islands. . . . At the time, the *Amoco Cadiz* incident resulted in the largest loss of marine life ever recorded after an oil spill. Two weeks after the accident, millions of dead mollusks, sea urchins, and other . . . species washed ashore. . . . Diving birds constituted the majority of the nearly 20,000 dead birds that were recovered. Oyster cultivation in the estuaries was seriously affected and an estimated 9,000 tonnes were destroyed because of contamination and to safeguard market confidence. Other shell and fin fisheries as well as seaweed gathering were seriously affected in the short-term, as was tourism.

International Tanker Owners Pollution Federation Limited (ITOPF). "Case Histories: A." www.itopf.com/information-services/data-and-statistics/case-histories/alist.html#atlantic.

Although the death toll and extensive property damage were unfortunate, the *Sansinena* disaster had two positive consequences. First, the incident resulted in improved tanker designs and procedures that no longer allowed rising vapors to mix with the air surrounding a docked ship. Second, the amount of oil that leaked into the environment was small compared to most other major tanker accidents.

The amount of oil spilled in the 1989 *Exxon Valdez* accident, for example—240,000 barrels—was eight times larger than the amount ejected in the *Sansinena* explosion. In the case of the *Exxon*

Valdez, human error—more specifically the insufficient experience and skill of the pilot—appeared to be the principal cause. An American University study cites how the calamity occurred:

> On board that night was Captain Joseph Hazelwood, a harbor pilot, and third mate Gregory Cousins. Once the harbor pilot had safely guided the huge vessel through Valdez Narrows and past Rocky Point he departed, and left the tanker in the command of Captain Hazelwood. . . . Before retiring to his cabin, Captain Hazelwood instructed his third mate Gregory Cousins to steer the vessel back into the southbound lane once it passed Busby Island. Although Cousins did give the instructions to the helmsman to steer the vessel to the right, the vessel was not turning sharply enough and at 12:04 A.M. the vessel hit Bligh Reef. It is not known whether Cousins gave the orders too late, the helmsman did not follow instructions properly, or if something was wrong with the steering system of the vessel. The impact was so forceful that it ripped through its cargo tanks, spilling tons of oil into the sound so quickly that it created waves of oil three feet above water level. All told, over 11 million gallons of oil leaked out into the Prince William Sound creating the worst oil spill in American history.[21]

Human error was also behind an even larger tanker accident that happened in March 1967 off the coast of England. The captain of the giant tanker *Torrey Canyon* made several gross navigational errors, causing the ship to run aground. About 775,000 barrels of petroleum, more than three times the amount spilled in the *Exxon Valdez* incident, poured into the sea.

Oil Rig Accidents

Disasters involving ocean-based (or offshore) oil rigs have the potential for releasing even more crude petroleum than do tanker accidents like those of the *Torrey Canyon* and *Exxon Valdez*. Oil rigs are big raft-like platforms loaded with drilling equipment. Such a drill creates an undersea oil well by penetrating

This April 27, 2010, NASA photo shows the Deepwater Horizon's oil slick in the lower right. The largest oil spill in history, approximately 5 million barrels of oil were released into the environment.

the ocean floor and tapping into a reservoir of oil. The reason that an oil rig can spill more oil than a tanker is that a tanker carries a set, limited amount of liquid cargo. In contrast, a typical oil reservoir contains dozens or even hundreds of times more oil than a tanker can carry. So when an oil rig mishap occurs, an almost unlimited amount of oil can escape into the sea before the wellhead or pipeline is fixed. This, of course, is what occurred in the 2010 Deepwater Horizon disaster in the Gulf of Mexico. The largest ocean-based oil spill on record, it leaked about 5 million barrels—almost six times more than the *Torrey Canyon* did—into the environment. As for the cause of the gulf accident, a January 2011 report by the online science journal *Bioscience Technology* states:

> A lack of safety procedures was identified by the oil spill investigation commission, set up by President Barack Obama, as a determining factor behind the disaster. The three companies involved in the accident—BP, Transocean, and Halliburton—were all accused of having cut corners in order to complete the well. At the time of the blow-out, this job was five weeks behind schedule. Five survivors talked to CNN about a corporate culture in which safety warnings were routinely ignored.[22]

Before the Deepwater Horizon incident, the worst oil platform disaster had been that of the Mexican-owned-and-operated Ixtoc I, a large rig in the Bay of Campeche (an inlet of the Gulf of Mexico). In June 1979 a loss of proper circulation in the drilling apparatus caused pressure to build up until a blowout (an uncontrolled release of crude oil) occurred. Some of the oil then ignited, creating a raging fire, and soon the platform collapsed. Before the well was capped almost a year later, oil had been escaping at a rate of 10,000 to 30,000 barrels a day. The total amount of petroleum spilled was approximately 3.5 million barrels.

The worst oil rig disaster from the standpoint of human lives lost was the destruction of the Piper Alpha platform in the North Sea in July 1988. When a pump failed, combustible gases escaped and ignited, producing an explosion and fire. Of the

229 men on the rig at the time, 167 were killed in the span of only a few minutes. Fortunately, the amount of oil leaked was minimal.

Intentional Releases of Oil

Tankers and oil rig disasters and other kinds of accidents are not the only events that spew petroleum into the environment. Many people are unaware that intentional dumps and leakages release a great deal of oil each and every year. Some of these purposeful discharges, known as "routine releases," are small-scale and cause only minor pollution of the seas. For example, maritime law permits tanker ships to periodically clean out their holds. To do this, their crews pump seawater in and then flush out the water-and-oil mixture. Some environmental groups have called for either a ban on such releases or a lowering of the amount of oil allowed to be dumped in each cleaning. For now the issue remains controversial, partly because oil companies claim that routine releases are the only practical means of cleaning the oil compartments.

THE PERILS OF OFFSHORE OIL

"Offshore oil imperils ecosystems, destroys livelihoods and undermines the economy. Offshore oil is inconsistent with a 21st century economy, particularly in light of the fact that clean energy can provide more jobs, less pollution, and real energy independence." —Richard Matthews, owner and author of *The Green Market* blog.

Richard Matthews. "Offshore Oil Is an Avoidable Tragedy." *Green Market*, May 14, 2010. http://thegreenmarket.blogspot.com/2010/05/offshore-oil-is-avoidable-tragedy.html.

Much more problematic and harmful are the illegal releases of petroleum each year. Unbeknownst to the general public, over the years some oil company owners have ordered the purposeful scuttling of their fully loaded tanker ships. Since a vessel and its oil are insured for large amounts of money, after the loss an owner collects a big payout and puts much of the reward in

Volunteers work to clean up some of the oil that contaminated 199 miles of the Brittany coastline in March 1978. The spill killed more marine life than any other spill in history to that point.

his pocket. Another shady tactic employed by ship owners consists of secretly and illegally getting around government rules and regulations in order to save money. This often has disastrous results; namely an increased number of tanker accidents and oil spills. Scholar and writer Dyan deNapoli explains:

> Many ship owners, to save money on taxes and insurance, and to avoid penalties, register their vessels in countries where the fees are lower, the regulations more lax, and the inspections substandard—if even existent.

These are called "open registries" or "flags of convenience," and it's very convenient for unscrupulous or greedy ship owners to register their vessels in some of these countries. Ships flying under certain flags may be poorly constructed and poorly maintained. Their crews may be improperly trained, overworked, and underpaid, [and] forced to work in unsafe conditions, leading to even more accidents. . . . While not all open registries are disreputable, there are some where the standards are laughable and the laws nonexistent. One shocking example was the Cambodian Shipping Corporation (in operation from 1994 to 2002), whose questionable activities and unsafe practices ultimately caused the registry to be shut down.[23]

Added to this growing menace has been the large number of ships targeted and sunk during wartime. According to deNapoli, in such cases

a cargo ship's fuel oil will leak into the surrounding waters as the ship goes down, and an oil tanker carrying millions of barrels of oil can cause a devastatingly large oil spill as it sinks. Even years after sinking, these ships littering the ocean floor continue to pose a threat to the environment. It is estimated that more than 8,500 commercial and naval vessels went down during World War II alone, carrying up to 20 million tons of oil and fuel with them to their watery graves. As time passes and corrosion takes its toll, this oil will be discharged into the world's oceans. These sunken ships are ticking time bombs, and it is impossible to predict when they will release their deadly caches of oil.[24]

Out of Dante's Inferno

All oil spills and leaks resulting from such attacks on tanker vessels pose serious environmental threats. Yet they pale in comparison to a single wartime assault that took place in 1991 during the first Persian Gulf War. History's largest and most destructive oil release, either intentional or unintentional, was the

Oil fields in Kuwait burn out of control in March 1991 as Saddam Hussein orders his troops to destroy over seven hundred oil wells.

result of an attack on a group of land-based oil wells (although some tankers anchored nearby were also targeted). It occurred after Iraqi dictator Saddam Hussein had invaded the small neighboring country of Kuwait and the United States and several of its allies had sent troops to liberate the Kuwaitis. Out of spite, and also to create fear and confusion, Saddam ordered his soldiers to wreck and burn more than seven hundred oil wells, some 85 percent of Kuwait's land-based drilling rigs. The oil fields burned out of control for almost ten months. More than 5 percent of the country's land was contaminated, an area in which some three hundred artificial lakes of oil formed as damaged wellheads belched forth streams of dark crude.

Meanwhile, the winds picked up much of the oil that did not burn. As a result, massive clouds made up of tiny droplets created a sort of petroleum fog that killed trees and animals and ruined many freshwater reservoirs over a region of hundreds of square miles. Former U.S. Marine Randy Hammond saw the awful results of the attack from an airplane and later said,

> Flying over the oil wells, it was like something out of Dante's Inferno [a medieval poem describing a journey through the horrors of hell], with thick, black oilfield smoke, a littered battlefield, burning tanks, aircraft flying around—very surrealistic. You almost had to slap yourself into reality to go out there and do your mission.[25]

The amount of oil released during the destruction of Kuwait's wells remains controversial and may never be known exactly. One reliable source estimates that from 380 to 520 million gallons (1,438 L to 1,968 L), or roughly 9 to 12 million barrels, of oil were unleashed. Needless to say, the damage was enormous.

Having surveyed this and the various other ways that unwanted petroleum enters the environment, the next step is to examine the equally diverse ways that waterways, land, and air are affected by such spills and releases.

CHAPTER 3

ENVIRONMENTAL IMPACTS

When news of a large oil spill spreads around the world via television, radio, newspapers, and other media, one word that is repeated over and over is *environment*. This is not surprising. Outside of the human death toll, if any, in an oil spill disaster, the most immediate concern is that the spilled petroleum might damage the surrounding environment in various ways.

Scientifically speaking, the diverse ways that spilled oil enters and affects the environment are collectively called that oil's "fate." In any release of crude petroleum, but especially in the larger ones, the fate of the oil is always complex. That is, various percentages of the oil from that spill will be absorbed into the environment in very different ways. For example, in the case of the explosion aboard an offshore oil rig in the 1979 Ixtoc disaster, some of the oil released caught fire, and an estimated 10,000 tons (9,072 t) of oil (65,000 barrels) burned at or near the site of the collapsed platform. As a result, a fraction of the burned petroleum dispersed in gaseous form into the air, polluting it. Meanwhile, another fraction of the burned oil became toxic ash that settled on towns and fields over a region of hundreds of square miles.

As for what happened to the fraction of the oil that did not burn in that mishap, some of it evaporated, causing more air pollution. More of it congealed and sank into the sea, causing numerous effects on marine creatures and their habitats. In addition, much of it ended up on nearby shorelines. After the Ixtoc calamity, approximately 66,000 tons (69,900t or 430,000 barrels) of slimy crude spread across the coasts of northern Mexico and nearby Texas. There the oil interacted in numerous ways, almost all of

Workers spray chemical dispersants on excess oil around the burning Ixtoc well in the Gulf of Mexico in August 1979. Approximately 430,000 barrels of oil fouled coastlines in Mexico and Texas.

them destructive, with the local beach sands, marshes, estuaries, and wildlife. In some cases an undetermined fraction of the petroleum that reaches the shore can sink into the water tables— the underground freshwater reservoirs that sometimes extend inland from the beaches—and make its way into the reservoirs that people tap into for drinking, bathing, and washing.

The fate of large quantities of oil that enter the environment is clearly complicated and potentially harmful. Moreover, even though experts have studied oil spills for decades, the spills' effects are difficult to predict with assurance. "Leading scientists can build a model for what they think is going to happen," marine biologist Myron Fischer points out. "But we may wake up the next morning and not know exactly what to expect."[26]

Effects on Oceans and Shorelines

Despite the complexity of the impacts of oil spills and the uncertainty in predicting their effects, scientists do have a basic understanding of what happens when a large amount of oil enters the environment. In cases of ocean-based spills, at first the oil spreads across the water's surface, forming a slick. If the surface is calm, the slick may remain cohesive or contained in one or two large sections for hours or even days. In contrast, if the sea's surface is choppy, the slick will rapidly break up into many smaller sections. As time goes on, these drift outward across areas of many square miles.

During the days and weeks following a big spill, the oil that started out on the surface can have a number of fates, several of which may occur simultaneously. Some of the crude will end up in the air, and some will sink below the surface. Another fraction of the crude will decompose, or break down, and become part of the food chain as microorganisms, or germs, eat it. According to Carolyn Embach, a scholar who specializes in the oil and energy industries,

> Oil that contains volatile organic compounds [chemicals that can have adverse effects on living things] partially evaporates, losing between 20 and 40 percent of its mass and becoming denser and [thicker] (i.e., more resistant to flow). A small percentage of oil may dissolve in the

water. The oil residue also can disperse almost invisibly
in the water or form a thick mousse [pudding-like mass]
with the water. Part of the oil waste may sink . . . and the
remainder eventually congeals into sticky tar balls. Over
time, oil waste weathers (deteriorates) and disintegrates
by means of photolysis (decomposition by sunlight) and
biodegradation (decomposition due to microorganisms).
The rate of biodegradation depends on the availability of
nutrients, oxygen, and microorganisms, as well as temperature.[27]

The spilled oil that does not evaporate and remains in the
ocean can do serious harm, especially to fish and other marine
animals. Depending on how much oil is present and its thick-
ness, fish and other small swimming and crawling marine creatures can be smothered, poisoned, or both. In the 1978 *Amoco
Cadiz* spill off the northwestern French coast, for instance, millions of mollusks and sea urchins died along with an estimated
9,000 tons (8,165 t) of oysters.

THE BP OIL SPILL: NO BIG DEAL?

"This [2010 BP] spill is the equivalent of less than a drop in an
Olympic-sized swimming pool. For all but a tiny bit of the Gulf,
it will be back to normal within a year."—Simon Boxhall, National
Oceanography Centre expert on marine pollution.

Quoted in Niall Firth. "Where Did All the Oil Go? U.S.Press and Scientists Admit That BP
Spill Is Vanishing Much Faster than Expected." *Mail Online* (London), October 13, 2010.
www.dailymail.co.uk/sciencetech/article-1298932/Was-Tony-Hayward-right-BP-oil-spill-
all.html.

In addition to these short-term effects, the spilled oil usually has long-term ones as well. For instance, if enough members of one or more local fish species die, the animals that
normally eat those fish lose their main food source, which
means that the regional food chain can be interrupted or even
destroyed. When this happens, these species may take a long
time to reestablish themselves in the area. Or they may never

return. Either way, local fisherfolk may no longer be able to make a living.

If the spill happens near land, which is often the case, some of the oil eventually reaches the shoreline. There it coats beach sand, gravel, rocks, plants, and wildlife habitats, contaminating them with the chemicals in the petroleum. Areas that were once teeming with clams, crabs, turtles, and other small living things can become virtual wastelands almost devoid of life. The oil can also contribute to beach erosion by smothering the root systems of plants. When these systems die the soil becomes looser and erodes faster, thereby changing the very contours of the local coastline.

Furthermore, while the oil is still in liquid form, it can, depending on how deep and dense the soil is, sink downward to local water tables.

A scientific study of this phenomenon conducted at Canada's University of Calgary reported that an

> analysis of core samples from [oil] spill sites of various ages and locations indicated that biodegradation [breakdown] of oil is extremely slow in the . . . soil. Theoretical predictions indicated that contaminated groundwater might extend in the direction of flow from less than one meter to several thousand meters from a spill, depending [on various factors]. It is concluded that some oil spills on land [or that spread onto shorelines] have the potential to pose long term threats to groundwater quality.[28]

Effects on Larger Animals

Even if local water supplies are not contaminated by a large oil spill, animals in the area invariably suffer. Studies show that fish, oysters, turtles, and other small creatures may die in large numbers. But they are not alone. Although they have the physical means to escape an area fouled by a spill, larger animals, such as dolphins, birds, otters, seals, and deer, often do not comprehend the danger in time. So they stay and end up as victims of the widening disaster.

Among these victims, birds are perhaps depicted most often in news reports and educational photos and videos depicting oil spills. When news coverage of the *Amoco Cadiz* incident revealed

Saving the Penguins

Jane Stanfield, an American from Denver, Colorado, went to South Africa to volunteer her services to the Southern African Foundation for the Conservation of Coastal Birds (SANCCOB). This is the organization that saved thousands of oil-soaked penguins in 2000. Stanfield here recalls some of the ways she and the other volunteers treated stricken birds.

Depending on the number of birds at the time, the closest pen to the main hospital held the birds that required the most medical treatments. When assigned this pen, in addition to cleaning and feeding duties, you could expect 2–3 treatment sessions daily. The treatments might include inserting stomach tubes to give water to the dehydrated birds, or Darrow's solution, which is essentially Gatorade for penguins. . . . Other treatments might include giving pills or putting the birds in a [special] box that misted medication for them. . . . Daily records were kept on each bird including medical treatments and number of fish eaten. Weekly, every bird at SANCCOB was weighed, blood tested, and evaluated for possible release. A bird was usually cleared for release when it weighed an appropriate weight for its age, had completely waterproof feathers, could swim at least one hour without wanting to come out of the water, and its blood was clear of malaria and [other diseases].

Jane Stanfield. "The Penguins of SANCCOB." www.transition abroad .com/listings/work/volunteer/ar ticles/volunteering-in-south-africa-with-penguins .shtml.

SANCCOB volunteers apply an antibiotic eye treatment to a young penguin's eyes. The Amoco Cadiz *spill killed nearly twenty thousand seabirds.*

that close to twenty thousand dead birds were found in the vicinity of the spill, the scope of the tragedy hit home. (Experts estimate that thousands more died, but their bodies were never recovered.)

The birds died as a result of a coating of petroleum on their feathers. When they attempted to clean themselves, they unwittingly ingested enough of the oil to poison and kill them. Also, many seabirds were adversely affected when the oil coating their feathers made them too heavy to fly. A number of those that had not yet died were rescued, cleaned, and released back into the wild. An observer familiar with the procedure for cleaning oiled birds writes,

> If workers have found sea birds that are not dead because of oil, they will take the birds to a cleaning center . . . where they are kept in a facility because they cannot live in the wild on their own. [They] will be cleaned by professionals and volunteers. When a bird is in captivity, the oil will be flushed from its eyes, intestines, and feathers. The bird will be examined for [other] injuries like broken bones, and it will [be given] medicine to prevent [sickness from any ingested oil]. After the bird seems healthier, it will take a test on its abilities to float in the water. . . . As soon as the bird passes its test, it will be let out into the wild.[29]

The largest and most famous effort to clean and save birds coated by petroleum after a big spill occurred in 2000. On June 3 of that year an ore-carrying vessel, the *Treasure*, sank off the coast of western South Africa. Most of the 1,344 tons (1,219 t) of heavy fuel oil, 56 tons (51 t) of diesel oil, and 64 tons (58 t) of lube oil it was carrying spilled into the surrounding waters. Unfortunately, the site of the disaster was also the location of the world's third largest colony of African penguins, an endangered species. The day after the accident the oiled birds began staggering ashore. As told by an eyewitness who later wrote a book about it, the bedraggled penguins

> were now landlocked. They could not return to the sea to hunt for food, because their soiled feathers no longer

A dead sea otter coated with crude oil from the Exxon Valdez oil spill lies on a beach in Prince William Sound. When covered in oil sea otters' temperatures drop rapidly, making them ill. They are prone to further injury when they try to rid themselves of the toxic oil.

provided protection from the icy waters. Any oil-coated penguins that were eventually driven by hunger to brave the waters to feed were quickly forced back to shore by the penetrating cold. Even though schools of fish were just yards away in the ocean, the penguins were compelled to stay on dry land. But standing there, they would soon starve to death. Their hungry chicks would starve as well. It was an impossible situation. There were no good options for the penguins [and] there seemed to be no way out of their deadly predicament.[30]

However, the confused and hungry creatures were not fated to die in that manner. Learning of their plight, a South African environmental group, the Southern African Foundation for the Conservation of Coastal Birds (SANCCOB), swung into action. It put out the word, and within hours some 12,500 volunteers from around the world were on their way to help. Working tirelessly, they fed, cleaned, and ultimately saved almost twenty thousand penguins.

UNDERWATER OIL PLUMES A HIDDEN DANGER

"Just because you don't see it on the surface or on the coast, it doesn't mean there isn't a problem. . . . If there are large plumes of oil underwater we might not be able to see [them] for some time."—Felicia Coleman, director of the Coastal Marine Laboratory at Florida State University.

Quoted in Eric Niiler. "Underwater Oil in Gulf Poses Threats." DiscoveryNews, August 3, 2010. http://news.discovery.com/earth/gulf-oil-spill-underwater-coasts.html.

These flightless birds had been on the verge of dying of hypothermia, a condition in which the body's temperature becomes too low for it to function normally. Numerous birds and other larger animals that have gotten caught in oil spills have died from that condition. Still others succumbed when oil they ingested reached their lungs or livers. Petroleum also causes the deaths of animals by blinding them. A creature that has lost its

Petroleum Invades an Aquarium

The oil spill that injured so many penguins after the sinking of the *Treasure* off South Africa's coast in 2000 also seeped into an aquarium on Cape Town's waterfront. Dyan deNapoli, one of the American volunteers who arrived to help the birds, later recalled:

> [The oil] had managed to infiltrate the aquarium's water collection system. [It] clogged filters and contaminated some of the water supply. The water filtration system was shut down while filters were changed and strips of absorbent cloth were put into the tanks to soak up the oil. The aquarium had to switch over to a closed water system which recirculates the same supply of water through biofilters. . . . Until all of the remaining oil had been cleared from the waterfront, the aquarium had to operate on this backup system.

Dyan deNapoli. *The Great Penguin Rescue.* New York: Free Press, 2010, p. 69.

sight is less able to detect the approach of deadly predators, which are likely to kill and eat it.

Cases of animals blinding themselves after being coated with crude oil have also been recorded. Some were sea otters. Normally energetic, playful creatures, when covered with petroleum their body temperatures drop rapidly, making them ill, listless, and lethargic. Desperate to rid themselves of the strange, dark substance, the creatures seriously maim themselves. Richard Newman, a California photographer who traveled to Alaska in 1989 to document the *Exxon Valdez* oil spill, later recalled his horror at finding a dead otter. "It tore up its own face," Newman said. "It scratched out its eyes because of the [oil]. It died with its paws folded on its chest." With a touch of sadness, he added, "another otter had chewed off a paw."[31]

Effects on Humans

A human who gets spattered with oil is not likely to chew off his or her own hand. Yet people, whose habitations are part of the overall earthly environment, are no less adversely affected by oil spills than animals are. In addition to the potential contamination of human water supplies, the oil can have other direct health effects on people. Breathing air polluted by gaseous oil compounds is unhealthy, for instance. So is prolonged skin contact with crude petroleum, as that toxic substance can be absorbed through the skin.

The dozens or even hundreds of people who spend days or weeks cleaning up a spill are commonly exposed to both spilled oil and noxious oil vapors. Thomas Webler and his colleagues at the Social and Environmental Research Institute in Greenfield, Massachusetts, write,

> Cleanup workers are potentially exposed to multiple toxins. They breathe fumes from oil and, even when issued protective clothing, gloves, and boots, they often end up with oil on their skin. One study found that among all cleanup workers, those who cleaned birds had the highest incidence of skin lesions from contact with oil (presumably because they removed their gloves so they could better clean the bird's feathers). . . . Documented health effects among cleanup workers in past [oil spill] events include both acute and chronic ailments, including headaches, nausea, skin rashes, long-term chemical sensitivity, ongoing dizziness, central nervous system damage, dermatitis, leukemia and other blood diseases, fetal defects, skin cancer, liver damage, damage to kidneys, [and] chronic respiratory tract irritation.[32]

Most people who live far from the sites of oil spills and are not involved in cleanup operations do not suffer from such direct toxic effects of petroleum. However, they can be potential victims of some indirect effects. One common example is by consuming fish or other animal products contaminated with oil from a spill. Some of the compounds found in petroleum can "bioaccumulate," or slowly build up, in a creature's body until they reach high concentrations. When a person eats the fish or other contaminated creature, he or she ingests the concentrated toxins.

Despite wearing protective clothing, oil spill cleanup workers are potentially exposed to multiple toxins that can cause skin lesions, headaches, skin rashes, central nervous system problems, and blood diseases.

Not every spill or release by itself is large and severe enough to seriously threaten animals, people, and the local environment they inhabit. So a single small spill or release in a given location may have only minor, temporarily harmful effects. As some experts point out, however, these incidents occur by the thousands worldwide each year, and their accumulated detrimental

Fish remain unsold in a Philippine market because of fear of contamination from a recent oil spill. When people eat contaminated fish they ingest concentrated toxins.

effects take a toll on the overall global environment. As expert observer Larry West puts it:

> Ultimately, the severity of environmental damages caused by [oil spills] depends on many factors, including the amount of the oil spilled, the type and weight of the oil, the location of the spill, the species of wildlife in the area, the timing of breeding cycles and seasonal migrations, and even the weather at sea during and immediately after the oil spill. But one thing never varies: oil spills are always bad news for the environment.[33]

ECONOMIC
IMPACTS

As one might expect, tens of thousands of news reports, articles, and commentaries were generated by the 2010 BP oil rig disaster in the Gulf of Mexico. Some described the event itself, including the loss of life and steady leakage of petroleum from the damaged wellhead. Others expressed worry about the environmental destruction that might occur along the gulf's coasts.

In addition, a large proportion of the reports and articles addressed the potential economic impact of the catastrophe. Typical was a July 2010 entry on the widely read *Huffington Post* news blog, which states,

> Almost three months after the explosion of the Deepwater Horizon rig in the Gulf of Mexico, the economic impact of the disaster continues to spread across coastal communities and beyond, destroying jobs and livelihoods, hurting businesses and damping tourism. Based on the experience of Alaskan communities after the *Exxon Valdez* disaster, the economic devastation is sure to be felt for decades and total billions of dollars. Though the impact at this stage is hard to measure and is bound to change . . . there are hundreds of towns and cities already suffering.[34]

This brief commentary summarizes some of the major economic consequences of large oil spills—loss of jobs, harmful effects on local businesses, and a decline in tourism. Among many others are short- or long-term financial expenses shouldered by the responsible oil companies, including cleanup costs, government fines, and settlements on lawsuits. These costs alone can

A Louisiana shrimper prepares locally caught shrimp for shipment to restaurants. The Deepwater Horizon oil spill devastated the gulf shrimp industry and caused severe economic hardship for members of the fishing industry.

run into billions of dollars. Another common effect is a reduction in property values in the towns in the affected area. This happens partly because of physical damage done by the oil and partly as a result of the damage done to a town's image in the eyes of the general public.

Another economic consequence consists of higher prices nationwide for products dependent on raw materials from the affected area. A clear example was a noticeable bump in the price of frozen seafood dinners in the wake of the BP disaster. After the accident, production of seafood in the gulf seriously declined. The sudden decrease in supply drove up costs for companies that package seafood for frozen dinners, a cost those companies passed along to consumers in the form of higher prices in retail stores.

Impacts on the Surrounding Region

Higher prices of various items in stores is only one of several little-known economic impacts following nearly all large-scale oil spills. Among the other industries that are adversely affected by such events are those that use a lot of seawater in their daily operations. For example, a number of big power stations use large quantities of seawater for cooling purposes. When the surrounding waters are fouled by petroleum, the slimy substance

Oil spills in harbors disrupt marine traffic and slow down or halt local import/export of goods.

can, to cite an old adage, gum up the works. This became a concern following the BP gulf spill, as explained by a spokesperson for *IEEE Spectrum*, a leading technology journal:

> Nineteen thermoelectric power plants on the coasts of Florida, Mississippi, and Texas suck in a total of 51 billion liters [11.2 billion gallons] of seawater per day, according to . . . the U.S. Energy Information Administration. The water piped into a plant is directed through thousands of metal tubes inside a condenser, where it cools and condenses steam from the plant's turbines. The condensed steam gets pumped back to the boiler to drive the turbine, and the heated saltwater flows back into the sea. Energy companies operating the plants worry that if [an oil] slick spreads to their intake canals, oil could get into the cooling machinery and potentially shut down the plant.[35]

The operators of desalination plants, which change seawater into freshwater, also worry about the occurrence of oil spills in their areas. Removing the oil from polluted water is both difficult and expensive, they say. Similarly, coastal facilities such as ports, harbors, and shipyards can be negatively affected by large oil slicks. The oil disrupts marine traffic in and out of harbors and, in turn, slows down or halts local import and export of various goods. The slicks also coat ship hulls, docks, and equipment, necessitating expensive cleanup operations.

Among the better-known economic outcomes of large ocean-based oil spills is the negative impact on nearby fisheries and fisherfolk. First, a sometimes serious loss of fish, clams, crabs, and other marketable marine animals occurs as a result of oil pollution. If local fishers cannot continue to catch and sell these creatures, they can suffer serious financial hardships. In the worst cases, they go bankrupt and can no longer make a living. The many Mexican fishers who had long plied their trade in the waters affected by the 1979 Ixtoc I disaster, for example, were financially devastated. It took several years for the local fish populations to replenish. Even worse, in some nearby areas the oysters were permanently eradicated. Journalist Mark Schrope, who investigated the Ixtoc incident, writes that the oysters "were

The Gulf Coast fishing industry was devastated by the Deepwater Horizon oil spill.

once so abundant that local fishermen say they could chop off a mangrove branch and pluck off enough of [them] to feed their families. The oysters never returned after Ixtoc I, according to the fishermen, and there is no research to explain why."[36]

Also, fishers who work in areas devastated by oil spills often suffer a loss of time and money when large-scale cleanup operations get in their way. Making matters worse, sometimes the local authorities impose a ban on fishing until the cleanup is over. In addition, the fishers frequently have to contend with damage done to their boats, nets, or other equipment by the oil. According to ITOPF,

An oil spill can directly damage the boats and gear used for catching or cultivating marine species. Floating equipment and fixed traps extending above the sea surface are more likely to become contaminated by floating oil, whereas submerged nets, pots, lines and bottom trawls are usually well protected provided they are not lifted through an oily sea surface.[37]

Loss of Tourism

Along with the harmful impacts on the fishing industry, one of the most visible and detrimental economic effects of marine oil spills (as well as spills on land) is the potential loss of tourism in the affected area. The activities that tourists normally engage in, such as swimming, boating, deepwater diving, lounging on the beach, recreational fishing, sightseeing, and so forth, can be curtailed by a large spill. If this situation lasts for months or longer, the local tourism industry can be devastated. Hotels, restaurants, gift shops, and other local businesses can suffer severe financial losses.

OFFSHORE DRILLING HAS BENEFITS

"At $50 per barrel, the [economic] benefits of offshore oil production in the formerly off limits areas of the outer continental shelf would garner $492 billion in revenues, $42 billion in lower oil prices, and reduce the cost of oil price disruptions by $42 billion, yielding total benefits of $578 billion. . . . Offshore oil drilling remains a risk well worth taking."—Ronald Bailey, science correspondent for *Reason* magazine.

Ronald Bailey. "Weighing the Benefits & Costs of Offshore Drilling." *Reason*, May 4, 2010. http://reason.com/archives/2010/05/04/weighing-the-benefits-costs-of.

This is exactly what happened in the wake of the 1978 *Amoco Cadiz* spill. Studies of the event's impact indicate that as many as 245,000 people who had planned to visit the coast of Brittany, in northwestern France, that year did not show up. Estimates of the resulting losses of revenue in the region vary. One suggests that local businesses were set back by as much as $80 million.

An Economic Wild Card

The loss of tourism and the money it brings into an area can be one of the most devastating effects of a large oil spill. In the case of the BP oil spill in the Gulf of Mexico in 2010, the nearby coastal areas and cities, including New Orleans, were seriously affected by this loss. According to a 2010 report commissioned by the U.S. Travel Association,

> [A] survey found that 26 percent of those who had plans to visit the state of Louisiana had postponed or canceled their trip. The June survey, which focused on relatively nearby visitor markets in Texas, Mississippi and Florida, found that 17 percent had postponed or canceled their planned vacation to Louisiana. Equally serious is the perception that this disaster will affect Louisiana for years to come.

> Nearly 80 percent of national respondents believed the disaster would impact the state for at least two years with nearly 40 percent stating that the impact will extend five years or longer. . . . This is the true wild card. Leisure travelers [tend to use caution when making] their choice of destination and may avoid regions which have only slight contamination or perhaps even the risk of oil. This can affect a destination for much longer than the disaster itself and may be the most significant factor in determining the eventual impact on the affected tourism economies.

U.S. Travel Association. "Potential Impact of the Gulf Oil Spill on Tourism." Prepared by Oxford Economics, pp. 8, 10. www.ustravel.org/sites/default/files/page/2009/11/Gulf_Oil_Spill_Analysis_Oxford_Economics_710.pdf.

When tourists tend to stay away from an area because of a recent oil spill, local leaders often try to lure them back. One of the more successful means has been the creation of television and magazine ads that downplay the spill's size and harmful effects. In such cases the oil company responsible for the spill sometimes pays for some or all of the costs of these ads. This is usually part of an attempt to rehabilitate the company's image while helping the locals with their financial recovery.

After the *Exxon Valdez* disaster in 1989, for example, the Alaskan tourism industry rapidly lost more than 26,000 jobs and some $2.4 billion in sales. Exxon reacted by spending $4 million on public relations efforts, including a popular ad campaign that drew a lot of attention. According to Art Davidson, an Alaskan who has written about that infamous spill,

> The ad agency chose the late movie star Marilyn Monroe over wolves, bears, or whales as a symbol for Alaska's environmental purity. The ads, which appeared nationally in both magazine and television versions, featured Marilyn's face without her beauty mark, the small mole on her cheek. The text, comparing Prince William Sound [where the spill took place] to Marilyn's mole, suggested that Alaska was just as beautiful without Prince William Sound as Marilyn Monroe would have been without her beauty mark. [The text stated that] "unless you look long and hard, you probably won't notice her beauty mark is missing." This peculiar conclusion [blended] seamlessly with Exxon's official story—that the situation just wasn't that bad.[38]

The success of this and other ad campaigns connected to the *Exxon Valdez* disaster was mixed. Many people, including residents of other states, liked the ads and appreciated that both Alaska and Exxon desperately wanted to improve their images. But by 2003 tourism in and around Prince William Sound had only moderately recovered. Moreover, in the years that followed, many out-of-state vacationers said they still thought of the region as polluted, despite years of cleanup efforts.

Costs of the *Exxon Valdez* Spill

The *Exxon Valdez* catastrophe, which until 2010 had held the record for the largest U.S. oil spill, had several other major long-term economic impacts. Among them were the monies Exxon itself had to spend on cleanup, government fines, and damages from lawsuits brought against the company by various groups and individuals. The initial cleanup costs were about $3.8 billion, equivalent to well more than $10 billion today. Also, because the tanker's grounding was declared a criminal act, Exxon was ordered to pay a fine of $150 million, then the largest fine ever imposed for an environmental crime. The company also

Members of the International Bird Rescue Research Center saved sixteen hundred birds and 334 sea otters contaminated by the Exxon Valdez *oil spill.*

paid out $300 million to eleven thousand Alaskan businesses and individuals to compensate them for losses incurred by the spill. In addition, it paid another $900 million over the course of ten years for other types of compensation.

COASTAL DRILLING IS A DISASTER!

"Apart from the terrible environmental damage caused by the Gulf spill, the economic costs are also enormous. . . . Shutting down coastal industries has huge indirect effects on suppliers, retailers, transport firms, etc. which will damage the wider economy and make all of us poorer."—The Debatabase Book, an online research source.

Debatabase Book. "Offshore Drilling." August 18, 2010. www.idebate.org/debatabase/ topic_details.php?topicID=1022.

Exxon was much more fortunate when it came to paying damages in the many lawsuits against it. According to Larry West, an authority on environmental policy,

> The *Exxon Valdez* oil spill led to many lawsuits. In 1994, an Alaskan jury ordered Exxon Mobil to pay $287 million in actual damages and $5 billion in punitive damages. In 2006, an appeals court reduced punitive damages for the *Exxon Valdez* oil spill to $2.5 billion, half the original amount. Two years later, in June 2008, the U.S. Supreme Court cut the punitive damages even more, to $507.5 million. The new figure represented about 12 hours of revenue for the giant oil company at the time of the ruling.[39]

The aftermath of the *Exxon Valdez* incident demonstrated another economic dimension of large-scale oil spills—the costs of rehabilitating animals oiled in the disaster. Part of Exxon's compensation payments went to restoring the environment in the damaged area. That included rescuing and cleaning animals and returning them to the wild. One of several rescue and rehabilitation efforts in Prince William Sound was that of the International Bird Rescue Research Center (IBRRC). Its operation, which utilized 143 boats, saved 1,600 birds and 334 sea otters. Exxon absorbed the cost of that effort as well as the costs of capturing and rehabilitating numerous other creatures native to the area.

These costs were considerable. At the time, an average zoo paid up to $50,000 to capture a single otter, and Exxon paid between $40,000 and $90,000 to rehabilitate each of the oiled otters that was captured. Each harbor seal that was rehabilitated cost the company $20,000, and each eagle caught and sent back into the wild cost $22,000. In the first week following the spill, Exxon spent more than $218 million on the rehabilitation of just four species—otters, sea birds, seals, and eagles. It later spent many millions more on members of other species that had gotten caught in the spill.

An even larger economic effect of the *Exxon Valdez* disaster consisted of the revenues lost when industries and businesses were hit hard in the pocketbook. Some even had to close. In the wake of the spill, for instance, the herring, salmon, shrimp, and crab fisheries in the region virtually shut down for more than a year. The costs of the lost resources, jobs, and opportunities—together often called "non-use value"—were and remain difficult to compute. But most experts place the total non-use value of the losses incurred by the spill somewhere between $4.9 billion and $7.2 billion.

The Financial Impact in the Gulf

With the exception of people who work in the oil industry and the residents of Alaska, by the start of 2010 most Americans had more or less forgotten about the *Exxon Valdez* disaster. But later that year, when BP's Deepwater Horizon rig burned and oil from its wellhead began gushing out, the earlier incident was once more in the news. Print articles and TV and radio commentators constantly compared the two accidents, including their economic impacts.

The total financial losses incurred by the BP gulf spill have not yet been fully tallied. However, some experts have offered general estimates of the losses suffered during the first year following the mishap. The costs to BP alone were at least $5 billion by February 3, 2011. That included cleanup costs, monies spent on ad campaigns to refurbish the company's tarnished image, and settlements of more than a thousand compensation claims by gulf residents and businesses. (Another fifty-seven hundred claims had been filed by that date but were yet to be settled.)

Others have begun studying and/or speculating about the potential long-term economic effects of the disaster. Late in 2010, for instance, the U.S Travel Association estimated that lost tourism could cost the gulf states as much as $23 billion between 2010 and 2013. Other predictions came from interviews with

Frustrated Gulf Coast residents attend a meeting to get information and assistance with the BP claims process. Claims rose to more than sixty-seven hundred against BP, but as of February 2011 the company has settled only about a thousand.

A Nation's Future Up in Flames?

The economic impact of the burning of the Kuwaiti oil fields in 1991, the largest single oil release in history, was huge by any standard. Donella H. Meadows, who taught environmental studies at Dartmouth College in New Hampshire, touched on part of that impact while it was happening:

> Some experts are saying three million barrels a day are burning in the desert. Some put the number at 1.5 to 2 million barrels, about the amount of oil Kuwait was producing before the war. We know . . . that at $20 a barrel Kuwait is losing about $60 million a day in revenues—$22 billion a year. The economic loss may be far greater than that, because the oil is being sucked out of the burning wells faster than the sustainable production rate, which is the rate at which underground oil can flow toward the wellhead. Pulling the oil out too fast means that subterranean salt water flows in to fill the breach. That makes the remaining underground oil harder to recover, maybe impossible to recover. We won't know for a long time how much the fires are reducing Kuwait's ultimately usable oil reserves [on which its economy is based].

Donella H. Meadows. "Kuwait's Oil—the Future Up in Flames." Sustainability Institute. www.sustainer.org/dhm_archive/index.php?display_article=vn382wellsed.

gulf-area politicians and business owners, conducted by MSNBC journalist Allison Linn. Summing up their worries about the long-term economic outlook in their region, she writes,

> The Gulf oil spill that is contaminating the waters off the coast of Louisiana could have an economic ripple effect extending to Florida and beyond, even if the slick doesn't cause extensive damage in those states. Just the fear that the oil slick will reach the coasts of Alabama, Mississippi, Florida or beyond is already discouraging some tourists from planning trips to those areas. . . . Concern over oil damage potentially could even put a

damper on coastal real estate markets, [and] in a worst-case scenario, the oil could cause billions of dollars in damage to property, wildlife, [human] livelihoods, and the seafood industry all along the southeastern edge of the United States and take several years to fully clean up. The problem is, nobody knows for certain whether the growing spill will cause such widespread harm.[40]

Linn and other investigators have heard forecasts of even more dire long-term economic impacts of the BP spill. These include thousands more Gulf Coast businesses closing down, tens of thousands of residents not being able to pay their mortgages, and possible foreclosures on and evictions from many of those houses. Still another worry is that, fearing more oil rig mishaps, the federal government might impose a temporary ban on deep-sea oil drilling, which could throw the thousands of people employed by the oil companies out of work. On the flip side, a number of economists and state officials say such predictions are alarmist. They insist it is too early to know whether any of these bleak scenarios will come to pass.

Most of the area's residents naturally hope the more optimistic estimates will be proven right. They know that only time will tell how extensive the damages wrought by the disaster will be. In the meantime, living with constant uncertainty about that future is difficult. The director of Florida's Institute for Economic Competitiveness told Linn: "Right now it's kind of like a hurricane spinning offshore, but it's not clear how and where and to what extent it's going to have an effect."[41]

CLEANING UP
OIL SPILLS

Only a few oil spills, both in water and on land, make it into newspapers, television broadcasts, and other media. Almost always they are the largest oil-related events. According to the EPA and other sources, they are the ones that exceed about 206,000 gallons (780,000 L) or roughly 4,900 barrels of petroleum spilled. These take place at a rate of about six or seven times a year world-wide. (They occurred an average of twenty-four times per year between 1970 and 1979. The reduction in the number of major spills in recent years is attributed to stricter safety regulations and improved tanker, rig, and pipeline designs.)

A hefty proportion of the coverage of these largest spills deals with the need to clean them up or the cleanup operations themselves. However, the fact that so few large-scale oil spills happen each year often gives the general public a misleading picture of the problem. Spills that release fewer than forty-nine hundred barrels occur by the thousands annually. In fact, the U.S. Coast Guard estimates that more than 250,000 oil spills took place in U.S. waters alone between 1971 and 2000. Many of these smaller events also require cleaning up. But because most of them are not heavily publicized, people living outside the affected areas (which includes most of the U.S. population) are unaware of these cleanup efforts. Most people are also unaware that all of the big oil companies have full-time professional cleanup crews and that together they keep thousands of cleanup workers busy on a regular basis.

Perhaps even more disquieting is the reality that a majority of the hundreds of oil cleanup operations that occur each year are largely ineffective. Indeed, despite the often herculean efforts

A sign warns people not to use Michigan's Kalamazoo River because of a recent oil spill. The Coast Guard says that more than 250,000 oil spills occurred in the United States between 1971 and 2000.

on the part of the oil companies, the Coast Guard, and other organizations, all of the existing cleanup methods are only partially effective. Much, and often most, of the spilled oil remains loose in the environment. Noted experts William R. Freudenburg and Robert Gramling wrote in 2011:

> We still really don't know how to clean up the oil that has been spilled into water bodies of any size. While the old adage is that oil and water don't mix, we have yet to

invent the techniques that can separate them, particularly after they are combined in significant quantities in large bodies of water. Oil spills are not new phenomena, but in no case—from the *Torrey Canyon* [spill in 1967] to the . . . *Deepwater Horizon* [spill in 2010]—has anyone ever been able to get more than about 5–10 percent of the oil back in the boat. That, moreover, is a generous estimate.[42]

Controlled Burns and Skimmers

One reason that most oil spill cleanups fail to get rid of the bulk of the oil is that when petroleum is released into the environment it spreads quickly. As a result, it reaches and pollutes numerous separate niches, variously including the air, ocean surfaces, ocean bottoms, shorelines, estuaries, marshes, woodlands, water tables, and many others. Just as no two of these settings are alike, no single cleanup method works in all of them. More times than not, multiple methods must be employed. Yet even then the oil frequently continues to spread, change consistency, and keep ahead of the earnest efforts of cleanup workers.

In short, when it comes to techniques for removing spilled oil from the environment, no magic bullet yet exists. The best that cleanup crews can do is to reach the spill site as soon as possible and remove as much of the oil as they can as quickly as they can. In this way, hopefully, they can contain much of it before it spreads far and wide and invades more environmental niches.

In the case of marine, or ocean-based, spills, the oil usually begins as a single or a few patches or slicks on the water's surface near the site of the spill. One way to attack such fresh slicks is to set them on fire. This is not as easy as it may sound, as the oil is constantly moving and breaking up into smaller slicks, all of them separated by seawater, which of course does not burn. Therefore, workers must first contain the slicks. They do this with long, tubelike barriers called booms. Made of rubber, plastic, or other materials, these float on the surface and become, in a sense, drifting fences that enclose one or more slicks. When the goal is to burn the oil, the workers employ fireproof booms. Once corralled, so to speak, the petroleum is set ablaze.

Though sometimes effective, such controlled burns are far from perfect solutions and have several disadvantages. First, to trap and burn all of the fast-spreading oil in a large spill is nearly impossible. Also, as pointed out in a special CNBC report on oil cleanup methods, controlled burns

> can be severely affected by bad weather. During the [2010 BP Gulf of Mexico] spill, controlled burn operations had to be postponed when waters made this technique dangerous. Controlled burns also produce columns of smoke, which shift the environmental impact from the sea to the air.[43]

The U.S. Coast Guard did end up burning some of the oil released in the BP gulf accident, particularly near the site of the ruined rig. However, the amount of oil disposed of in this manner was minuscule when compared with the overall size of the spill.

When using controlled burns is impractical or too dangerous, cleanup crews still employ booms to contain the oil. But instead of setting it ablaze, they try to suck the oil out of the containment area, a technique called skimming. A number of different kinds of skimmers are in standard use. Rope skimmers, for example, consist of ropelike belts that are very porous. When workers toss such a belt onto the surface of the contained slick and move the belt back and forth, some of the oil seeps into it and collects inside. Once the belt is saturated, the workers can throw in a fresh belt or use a different kind of skimmer.

One skimmer that is commonly used, especially in larger oil spills, is called a vacuum, or suction, skimmer. As the name suggests, one expert observer writes,

> suction skimmers operate similarly to a household vacuum cleaner. Oil is sucked up through wide floating heads and pumped into storage tanks. Although suction skimmers are generally very efficient, they are vulnerable to becoming clogged by debris and require constant

Workers aboard an oil skimmer scoop up tar balls in the Gulf of Mexico.

skilled observation. Suction skimmers operate best on smooth water, where oil has collected against a boom or barrier.[44]

Still another type of skimmer is the floating disk. The technology employs several partially submerged disks, most often made of aluminum or plastic. As these spin around within the slick, oil collects on their surfaces until workers stop and scrape the crude off into a collection tank. Like other kinds of skimmers, floating disks do not work well in choppy waters or strong, fast-moving tides. In those cases workers must resort to other cleanup methods.

Sorbents and Dispersants

Among those alternate cleanup techniques for marine spills is the use of sorbent materials, various substances that effectively absorb petroleum. Because sorbents, like the oil itself, disperse into and follow the currents, they are often effective in rough, rapidly shifting seas. Three kinds of sorbents are presently in use. One consists of natural inorganic (nonliving) materials such as sand, clay, and volcanic ash. Scientists have found that sorbents can absorb between four and twenty times their weight in oil.

Dispersants Can Be Effective

"When used appropriately, dispersants can be an effective method of response to an oil spill. They are capable of rapidly removing large amounts of certain oil types from the sea surface."—International Tanker Owners Pollution Federation Limited (ITOPF).

International Tanker Owners Pollution Federation Limited. "Dispersants." www.itopf.com/ spill-response/clean-up-and-response/dispersants/.

The second kind of sorbent includes natural organic (life-based or once-living) substances. Those most often employed in oil spill cleanups are sawdust, straw, peat moss, hay, ground corncobs, and feathers. According to oil spill expert Mallory Nomack,

> Organic sorbents can adsorb [adhere to their surfaces] between 3 and 15 times their weight in oil, but there are disadvantages to their use. Some organic sorbents tend to adsorb water as well as oil, causing the sorbents to sink. Many organic sorbents are loose particles such as sawdust, and are difficult to collect after they are spread on the water. These problems can be counterbalanced by adding flotation devices, such as empty drums attached to sorbent bales of hay, to overcome the sinking issue, and wrapping loose particles in mesh to aid in collection.[45]

The Controversy over Dispersants

The use of chemical dispersants is controversial, and a number of experts argue that they succeed only in breaking up a toxic substance into smaller pieces. Mallory Nomack, who has closely studied oil spills and their cleanup methods, elaborates.

> Dispersants have not been used extensively in the United States because of possible long term environmental effects, difficulties with timely and effective application, disagreement among scientists and research data about their environmental effects, effectiveness, and toxicity concerns. New technologies that improve the application of dispersants is being designed. The effectiveness of dispersants is being tested in laboratories and in actual spill situations, and the information collected may be used to help design more effective dispersants. Dispersants used today are less toxic than those used in the past, but long term cumulative effects of dispersant use are still unknown.

Mallory Nomack. "Oil Spill Control Technologies." Encyclopedia of the Earth, September 8, 2010. www.eoearth.org/articles/view/158385/?topic=50366.

A plane drops dispersants near the Deepwater Horizon oil spill. The use of dispersants is controversial because their long-term effects on the environment are unknown.

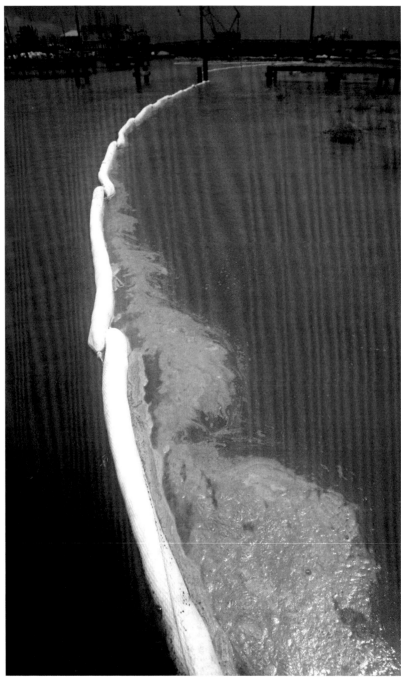

A sorbent boom stretches along a Gulf Coast shoreline. Made of rubberlike material, the booms absorb up to seventy times their weight in oil.

The third type of sorbent is synthetic, or human-made. The most common synthetic sorbents are rubberlike materials, which swell a great deal as petroleum penetrates them; polymers (long chains of molecules); and plastic-based substances such as polyurethane. When available, these can be highly effective because they absorb up to seventy times their weight in oil. In contrast, the chief drawback of all sorbents is that they must be collected and disposed of after they have done their work, a job that takes much time, energy, and money.

A second cleanup method that works well in choppy waters is the use of chemicals, often called dispersants. These substances break up, or disperse, the oil slick into billions of small droplets. In many cases, this makes the effects of the spill less

A Major Cleanup in Wales

The ITOPF's extensive online information sources on the history and impact of oil spills contain this summary of the cleanup of the *Sea Empress* spill in 1996.

[The] *Sea Empress*, carrying 130,000 tons of . . . crude oil, ran aground in the entrance to Milford Haven, Southwest Wales. . . . The [cleanup operations] included dispersant spraying, mechanical recovery [picking up the oil using skimmers and containers], and the use of the protective booms. This, coupled with a high rate of evaporation and natural dispersion, greatly reduced the quantity of oil reaching inshore waters. Some 200km of coastline, much of it in a National Park, was con-

taminated and a major shoreline cleanup effort had to be mounted, involving mechanical recovery [this time by hand and shovel], trenching, beach washing, and the use of dispersants and sorbents. . . . A temporary ban was imposed on commercial and recreational fishing in the region and there was concern that tourism, important to the local economy, would be badly affected by the heavily oiled beaches. Several thousand oiled birds washed ashore, leading to a major cleaning and rehabilitation operation.

International Tanker Owners Pollution Federation Limited (ITOPF). "Case Histories: S." www.itopf.com/information-services/data-and-statistics/case-histories/slist.html.

threatening and destructive to nearby coasts. However, scientists still debate whether using dispersants is a good idea. Some argue that these chemicals do not dissolve an oil slick; rather, they only break it down into smaller units, which remain in and can build up in the seas over time. Because of such concerns, the use of dispersants has been limited in U.S. coastal waters and is rarely used in inland lakes and ponds.

DISPERSANTS ARE A WITCH'S BREW!

"Dispersants . . . leave behind a witch's brew of other potentially-dangerous chemicals after interacting with crude oil in water. Not only do these toxic components damage the environment, but they introduce potentially-serious human health and marine environmental problems."—Toxicologist William Sawyer and attorneys Stuart Smith and Mike Stag.

William Sawyer, Stuart Smith, and Mike Stag. "Dispersants Used in Oil Disaster a Witch's Brew of Dangerous Chemicals." mfrtech.com, July 31, 2010. www.mfrtech.com/articles/3701.html.

Worries about the use of dispersants surfaced again in 2010 when 770,000 gallons (2.9 million L) of dispersants were dumped in the Gulf of Mexico to counteract the huge oil release from the wellhead of the BP rig. The results were mixed. Critics say that the chemicals were only marginally effective and complain that these toxic substances may eventually end up polluting the local food chain. In comparison, experts who favor the use of dispersants point out that they have been applied with a fair amount of success in Europe and elsewhere in the world with minimal negative effects.

A Biological Approach

Still another approach to cleaning up oil spills, one that may eventually replace chemical dispersants, is the use of biological agents. These are germs that have long existed in nature and that eat and digest petroleum. "You and I eat steaks and pizza, [while] microbes eat hydrocarbons,"[46] says Steve Kennedy, director of

Bioremediation, Inc., a company that employs germs to clean up toxic chemicals, including spilled oil. Kennedy points out that cleanup crews tested the technique during the 1989 *Exxon Valdez* spill in Alaska and in a number of smaller oil spill cleanups in the years that followed. Its principal benefit, he adds, is that it is not harmful to the environment. This is because the microbes it uses already exist in nature and are merely harvested, added to fertilizer or some other delivery material, and released back into nature.

The main problem with the biological approach is that germs take a long time to consume large-scale oil spills, apparently several decades to eradicate even a moderate amount of oil. So their use is not a quick fix. Also, in the oceans, where

Matter of Trust used booms full of human and animal hair to absorb spilled oil.

water is constantly moving, the microbes easily disperse before their job is done. That is why the biological method seems to work better for land-based spills and petroleum from marine spills that has already washed ashore.

Also, critics say, the fact that oil-eating germs work so slowly means that adding extra microbes to a large spill may be largely ineffective. Such germs were unleashed in the Gulf of Mexico in 2010, for instance. But so far their effects, along with those of the oil-consuming microbes that were already in the gulf, have been minimal. "Adding foreign microorganisms [germs] did not accelerate the naturally occurring process by which native populations of bacteria degrade oil in water,"[47] writes Sandra Upson, of *IEEE Spectrum*.

Green Solutions

This is not to say that using germs to eat spilled oil will never be practical. In fact, many scientists foresee that the biological method will become more effective in the near future as scientific advances speed up the process and make it more controllable. Certainly all experts agree that one extremely attractive aspect of the technique is that it is "green," or environmentally friendly. Finding other green technologies for cleaning up oil spills is already a priority for a number of small, emerging companies.

Among these new technologies is a superabsorbent organic peat moss developed by a small Norwegian company. Inhabitat, a New York City firm that tracks emerging advances in technology, describes how the substance works:

> The peat is scattered on the spill and absorbs the oil, and, because it doesn't absorb water, it can then simply be scooped out—taking the toxic oil with it. [The company's] staff members work with peat moss for gardeners, but when they observed how absorbent this particular type was, they started looking for other uses. The Norwegian government then got interested and tried using the peat moss to clean up an oil spill that was washing up on protected land. It worked [exceptionally well].[48]

Another proposed green solution for cleaning up petroleum spills comes from a San Francisco–based company, Matter of Trust. It consists of collecting large amounts of human and pet hair. The hair is stuffed into nylon leggings and made into absorbent mats that cleanup workers lay atop the surface of an oil slick. After the mats have soaked up the oil, they are picked up and discarded.

More innovative, experimental methods for removing spilled oil include agents that when spread on the liquid crude cause it to turn into solid, floating blocks that can easily be dragged or carried away; a device that sucks up the polluted water and spins the oil-and-water mixture at high speeds, separating the two and dumping the de-oiled water back into the ocean; and a giant geodesic dome that would be lowered onto a damaged wellhead (such as the one in the 2010 BP spill), thereby trapping the gushing oil inside.

Whether these particular ideas and inventions will ever be widely used is unknown. More certain is the fact that the existing standard cleanup methods are unable to clean up all the oil in a large or even moderate-sized spill. So new technologies to address the problem are seriously needed. One encouraging sign that that need will ultimately be met took place in July 2010. Inspired by the recent BP disaster, the X Prize Foundation, a California-based educational organization dedicated to creating a better future for humanity, offered a $1 million prize to be awarded to the person or group who comes up with the most promising new oil spill cleanup method.

PREVENTION OF
OIL SPILLS

Scientists, government officials, and members of the public all concur that applying vigorous cleanup measures to oil spills and finding improved technologies to do that important job are both vital. Yet also widely agreed upon is that preventing oil spills in the first place is even more desirable. Of course, no one believes that 100 percent of these mishaps can be avoided. Indeed, the consensus of experts is that as long as humans continue to use petroleum as a major energy source, at least occasional spills will be inevitable.

Undoubtedly the best-case scenario would be to replace oil with cleaner, less toxic energy alternatives. But experts say the practical reality is that humanity is still at least a few decades away from achieving that dream. In the meantime, they add, the oil companies, government agencies, and the public can work together to reduce the amount of oil that unnecessarily enters the global environment.

Stricter Environmental Laws

Experience has shown that one way to attain the challenging goal of reducing oil spills is through stricter regulation of the oil industry. Before the 1970s, for example, the U.S. government had made very few rules governing the drilling, storage, and transportation of petroleum. The principal reason for this lax policy was that most legislators thought restricting big oil companies too much would induce them to produce less oil. Then came a series of huge oil spills, including one in Santa Barbara, California, in 1969 and the *Argo Merchant* disaster in 1976. It became clear that the oil companies had done a poor job of policing themselves and that more effective government regulations were needed.

In this way, oil spills, coupled with the worsening of other environmental hazards, especially air pollution, inspired more than two decades of enthusiastic environmental activism in the United States. In December 1970 Congress created the EPA, and in 1977 it passed the Clean Water Act. Similarly, the 1989 *Exxon Valdez* spill prompted the passage of the most direct and restrictive regulatory assault on oil spills, the 1990 Oil Pollution Act (OPA).

The OPA established many new rules designed to make oil spills less likely to happen and less destructive when they did occur. For instance, the bill requires the Coast Guard to impose stronger regulations on oil tankers and their owners. One of these rules states that each oil company must find ways to better contain petroleum both in storage facilities and during transport of the substance. Companies are also required to devise comprehensive cleanup plans to implement in the advent of a spill. Furthermore, the OPA says that oil companies are responsible for oil

A U.S. Coast Guard team prepares to board and inspect an oil tanker in Chesapeake Bay. The Oil Pollution Act of 1990 requires the Coast Guard to impose stronger regulations on oil tankers and their owners.

removal costs and must pay fines for releasing oil into U.S. rivers
and coastal waters.

That such tougher regulations worked became clear when
the number of oil tanker disasters and large oil spills decreased
substantially in the 1990s and first decade of the twenty-first
century. Moreover, compelling the oil companies to take full financial liability (responsibility for paying) for most cleanup
costs of spills saved the federal government and local communities a great deal of money. This was evident during the 2010
BP spill in the Gulf of Mexico. Many people unfamiliar with the
1990 OPA were surprised to see BP executives publicly ensuring
the public that they would reimburse communities and individuals for their losses. The main motivations for this display of
goodwill were provisions in the OPA such as:

> Each responsible party for a vessel or a facility from which
> oil is discharged . . . into or upon the navigable waters or
> adjoining shorelines [of the United States] is liable for the
> removal costs and [financial] damages . . . that result from
> such incidents. . . . The removal costs [consist of] dam-
> ages for injury to, destruction of, loss of, or loss of use of,
> natural resources, including the reasonable costs of as-
> sessing the damage . . . [and] damages for injury to, or
> economic losses resulting from destruction of, real or per-
> sonal property, which shall be recoverable by a claimant
> who owns or leases that property.[49]

Improved Tankers and Drilling Procedures

Another approach to the prevention of oil spills has been an ongoing attempt to find safer and more efficient designs for oil-
carrying vehicles, especially large tanker ships. Before 1990
almost all tankers had single hulls. That is, all that stood between
a vessel's oil storage compartment and the ocean, river, or lake
waters beyond was a single one-and-a-half-inch layer of steel.
"When tankers with one shell are ruptured," one article on oil
spills remarks, "the only place for the oil to go is into the sea."[50]

That carrying petroleum in tankers with double hulls would
be a good deal safer was clear to the experts. For that reason, a

The oil tanker Polar Endeavour *is one of the new double-hulled oil tankers built to comply with regulations in the Oil Pollution Act.*

provision requiring the oil companies to switch from single-hulled to double-hulled tankers was inserted in the 1990 OPA. The newer vessels typically have an open space measuring from 6 to 10 feet (2 m to 3 m) thick between the two hulls. Thus, if the outer hull ruptures, the inner hull provides a second line of defense, and the toxic cargo remains intact. In June 1999 Coast Guard rear admiral Robert C. North testified before Congress on the impressive success of the OPA, including the ongoing adoption of double-hull designs for oil tankers. He stated,

> [The 1990 OPA] was truly an imposing piece of legislation. It required changes in virtually every aspect of the oil transportation industry. It involves new construction requirements, operational changes, response planning, licensing and [crew-related] mandates, and increased liability limits. . . . A significant pollution prevention standard in [the] OPA is the requirement for new tankers to be of double hull construction. This provision also required that existing single hull tank vessels be retrofitted with a double hull [i.e., have another hull added to the existing one] or, beginning in 1995, be phased out of

operation by 2015. . . . The double hull requirements were mandated to prevent, as far as practicable, any spills from occurring in U.S. waters. As stated in our 1992 report, the double hull was unmatched in preventing the majority of oil spills when compared to the proposed alternatives. None of those alternatives or the alternatives evaluated since can match the superior performance of the double hull regarding . . . oil outflow for both collisions and groundings.[51]

North went on to say that the double-hull design had definitely reduced the incidence of large oil spills like that of the *Exxon Valdez*. Seattle Coast Guard investigator Larry Lockwood, who had closely observed the performance of double-hulled tankers, had expressed the same enthusiasm for the double hull in 1990. "Almost without exception," he said, "if a ship has a double bottom you don't have a spill, and if it doesn't have a double bottom, you do. It doesn't take [the old popular comic strip detective] Dick Tracy to figure that out."[52]

THE FUTURE LIES IN GREEN ENERGY

"Clean energy sources, such as a combination of biomass, wind, solar and others (nuclear included), can begin to replace oil in our economy if the government directs incentives toward their use. Clean, green, renewable energy is the way of the future."—Chris Jordan, columnist.

Chris Jordan. "BP Oil Spills Show We Should Go Green Quickly." *The Daily of the University of Washington*, May 19, 2010. http://dailyuw.com/2010/5/19/bp-oil-spills-show-we-should-go-green-quickly.

Tankers are not the only oil-related apparatuses that have been targeted for improvement. Following the 2010 BP spill, industry experts, government officials, and critics in the media all recognized the need for ways to keep floating oil platforms and their drilling gear safer. Some of these observers have advocated better inspection procedures and more effective ways for

A More Efficient Cargo Hold

Several alternative designs for double-hull tanker ships have been advanced. Among them is the "American Underpressure System" developed by MH Systems of San Diego, California. The accompanying diagram and explanation, supplied by the company, show how it would work.

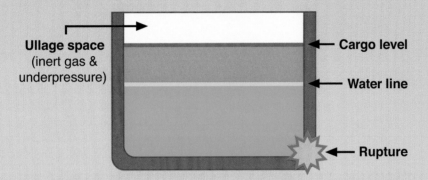

According to MH Systems's director, Mo Husain:

The underpressure concept is best understood by making an analogy with which most people can identify. Imagine sipping water half-way up through a straw and sealing off the top of the straw with your fingertip. A simple principle of hydraulics allows the water to be held in the straw at this level until the finger is released.

This same principle allows oil to be contained within the hull should a rupture occur in the tank. When a tanker is loaded, the oil level inside the tank is higher than the surrounding seawater level. This causes a higher pressure to exist inside the tanker. . . .

The system equalizes the pressure inside and outside the tanker at the rupture point by applying a slight underpressure . . . in the ullage space of the tank [the space above the oil's top level]. As oil flows out, it is replaced by seawater up to the rupture point only. Oil loss is held to a minimum as all oil above the rupture point will remain in the tanker.

Taken from: Mo Husain. "Full Scale Test of the American Underpressure System (AUPS) on Board the USNS Shoshone." MH Systems. http://www.mhsystemscorp.com/tech5.html.

Environmental groups' recommendations to cut back on gasoline use include carpooling, using public transportation, or riding a bicycle to work or school.

crews to detect faulty equipment and impending explosions. Others have suggested implementing improved wellhead designs that would make petroleum leaks less likely to occur.

Still another recommended approach to preventing oil rig disasters like the one in 2010 entails putting into practice a different procedure for drilling relief wells. Part of the ultimate capping of the broken BP wellhead involved drilling two other wells near the broken one in order to draw off much of the upwelling oil. Some critics say that this operation was executed too late. According to Marshall Brain, founder of the online information source HowStuffWorks,

> The problem with relief wells is time. It will take BP two to three months to get the first relief well in place. This is not the first time an oil well had sprayed millions of gallons of oil into the ocean, and it will not be the last unless we develop regulations to prevent it. . . . The obvious question going forward is: How do we prevent this situation from ever happening again? [One] solution [is that] we require drilling companies to drill their relief wells first, before they strike oil. Then, if there is a problem with the

main well, the relief wells are already in place and can be activated in a few hours rather than a few months.[53]

Less Dependence on Oil

One highly effective way of preventing oil spills is to use less oil in the first place. A number of scientists predict that in the near future a major goal of the United States, the United Kingdom, Canada, Japan, and other industrialized nations will be to reduce their dependence on oil for energy. The incidence of oil

A Matter of Apples and Oranges

Researcher and writer Thomas Ajava argues here that choosing between oil and solar power for energy is a matter of "apples and oranges."

Solar power primarily provides two types of energy. The first is electricity and the second is water heating. Solar panel systems are used to generate either of these forms of energy. There are larger commercial scale power plants based on solar energy, but they are few and far between. . . . As a burnable energy source, [oil] is primarily refined to create fuel for vehicles. These range from your average family car to jumbo jets flying around the world. The problem with the solar versus oil argument should be obvious. Solar will never replace gasoline and gasoline is not used as a fuel source to generate electricity in all but a few power plants. Coal is by far the most common fuel used to generate electricity. Solar might replace it one day, but that is an entirely different argument. Okay, what about solar cars? They are a nice idea, but we currently do not have the technology to make them happen nor will we for decades into the future. [So] the next time you hear the solar power versus oil heat up, you might want to mention the inherent problem with the debate.

Thomas Ajava. "Can Solar Power Replace Oil Consumption?" http://ezinearticles.com/?Can-Solar-Power-Replace-Oil-Consumption?&id=4668391.

spills should decrease as a result. Then, at an undetermined time after that, the hope is to largely replace oil with alternate energy sources.

To work toward the first of these goals—using less oil—ordinary people can significantly aid scientists and industry. Almost all people are consumers of oil-based energy sources like gasoline, for example. So if they consciously use smaller amounts of gasoline, they can collectively make a dent, so to speak, in the enormous demand for petroleum. An online bulletin from NOAA explains the individual citizen's place in the larger scheme of society and its dependence on oil:

> When we use less oil, less needs to be transported, and there's a lower risk of future oil spills. We should understand that it is because we rely on oil that we run the risk of oil spills. That means that all of us share both the responsibility for creating the problem of oil spills and the responsibility for finding ways to solve the problem.[54]

As for what individual citizens can do to help solve that monumental problem, NOAA and other environmental agencies and groups recommend making different choices in various aspects of their lives. To cut back on gasoline use, for instance, people can, where possible, carpool or use public transportation to get to work. Or if someone lives close enough, he or she can bicycle to work a couple of times a week or more.

Many other choices that reduce oil use can be made when shopping. Because many kinds of plastic are made from petroleum, one can, whenever possible, purchase products that are not packaged in plastic. That includes avoiding bottled water. (Reusing and/or recycling plastic containers is also helpful.) In addition, pesticides and fertilizers are mostly made from petroleum, so one can buy organic vegetables and fruit, which are grown without pesticides and fertilizers. Buying locally farmed produce helps, too. Because it does not have to be shipped from faraway places, it saves on gasoline and other fuels for trucks, ships, and other forms of transport. Another good idea is to read the labels on shampoos, soaps, and makeup products. Many contain oil, and versions made without oil are available.

Using alternate energy sources, which many people hope will eventually replace most of the oil employed in energy production, can also reduce dependence on petroleum. Some experts and others advocate expanding the use of nuclear power plants, of which a number have been in operation for a few decades. Presently around 440 nuclear plants exist in the world and produce 16 percent of the planet's electricity. (The United States has just over 100 such plants, which account for roughly 20 percent of the nation's power.) Advocates of nuclear power point out that these facilities create practically no air or water pollution and are safe if built and maintained properly. In contrast, critics of nuclear plants argue that they are very expensive to construct and maintain. Also, the nuclear wastes they generate are extremely toxic and difficult to store.

OIL WILL NOT BE REPLACED SOON

"Oil will remain the world's main source of energy for many years to come, even under the most optimistic of assumptions about the development of alternative technology."—International Energy Agency (IEA).

International Energy Agency. "New Energy Realities: WEO Calls for Global Energy Revolution Despite Economic Crisis." Press release, November 12, 2008. www.iea.org/press/pressdetail.asp?press_rel_id=275.

Much more attractive, those critics say, is the idea of producing energy via wind, solar, and geothermal sources. In this view, solar cells, which convert sunlight into electricity, are 100 percent clean and safe, while solar panels can heat air or water inside houses and other structures. Meanwhile, wind power can create electricity and has been shown to be safe, pollution free, and renewable. Still another popular green choice for energy production, geothermal power, which utilizes existing heat rising from the earth's core, is also renewable and relatively clean. Other clean, abundant energy alternatives that might be developed in the future include orbiting satellites that can capture solar energy

This house uses wind power, solar heat collectors, and photovoltaic panels. Dependence on petroleum can be reduced by using these alternative energy devices.

and relay it to the earth's surface and a controlled version of nuclear fusion, the process that makes the sun and other stars shine.

Whether any one or a combination of these sources will be able to effectively replace petroleum as a major energy source remains unknown. But one thing is certain. If and when that happens, big oil spills caused by human activity and the environmental threats posed by such spills will become a thing of the past.

Introduction: A Serious Ongoing Threat

1. Bob Cavnar. *Disaster on the Horizon: High Stakes, High Risks, and the Story Behind the Deepwater Well Blowout.* White River Junction, VT: Chelsea Green, 2010, pp. 12–13.
2. U.S. Environmental Protection Agency, Office of Emergency Management. "Threats from Oil Spills." www.epa.gov/oem/content/learning/effects.htm.
3. Climate Progress. "Exclusive: The Human Dimensions of Oil Spills." http://climateprogress.org/2010/05/05/human-dimensions-bp-oil-spill/.
4. U.S. Environmental Protection Agency, Office of Emergency Management, "Threats from Oil Spills."

Chapter 1: Why the World Uses So Much Oil

5. Sheryl Joaquin. "Petroleum—Its Uses and Benefits." Ezine Articles. http://ezinearticles.com/?Petroleum---Its-Uses-And-Benefits&id=775224.
6. Jeremy Leggett. "What They Don't Want You to Know About the Coming Oil Crisis." *Independent* (London), January 20, 2006. www.independent.co.uk/environment/what-they-dont-want-you-to-know-about-the-coming-oil-crisis-523830.html.
7. Anna Wegis. "A World of Petroleum." *Illumin.* http://illumin.usc.edu/article.php?articleID=59.
8. Herodotus. *The Histories.* Trans. Aubrey de Sélincourt. New York: Penguin, 1996, p. 431.
9. Herodotus, *The Histories,* p. 113.
10. Peter James and Nick Thorpe. *Ancient Inventions.* New York: Ballantine, 1994, pp. 405–406.
11. Marco Polo. *A Description of the World,* published as *The Travels of Marco Polo.* London: Folio Society, 1999, pp. 17–18.

12. Brian Black. "Petroleum History, United States." In *Encyclopedia of the Earth*, December 18, 2007. www.eoearth.org/article/Petroleum_history,_United_States.
13. Laura De Angelo. "Titusville, Pennsylvania." In *Encyclopedia of the Earth*, June 14, 2007. www.eoearth.org/article/Titusville,_Pennsylvania.
14. Oracle Education Foundation. "Oil Spills." http://library.thinkquest.org/CR0215471/oil_spills.htm.
15. Leggett, "What They Don't Want You to Know About the Coming Oil Crisis."
16. U.S. Environmental Protection Agency. "The Exxon Valdez Oil Spill: A Report to the President." www.epa.gov/history/topics/valdez/04.htm.

Chapter 2: The Causes of Oil Spills

17. S.E. Smith. "What Causes Oil Spills?" Wise Geek. www.wisegeek.com/what-causes-oil-spills.htm.
18. Auke Visser. "Collision of *Atlantic Empress* and *Aegean Captain*." www.aukevisser.nl/supertankers/part-1/id704.htm.
19. National Oceanic and Atmospheric Administration: Office of Response and Restoration. "Oil and Chemical Spills." http://response.restoration.noaa.gov/faq_topic.php?faq_topic_id=1.
20. NOAA Incident News. "*Sansinena*, Los Angeles Harbor, California." National Oceanic and Atmospheric Administration. www.incidentnews.gov/incident/6232.
21. American University. "*Exxon Valdez* Disaster." Trade and Environment Database (TED). www1.american.edu/TED/exxon.htm.
22. *Bioscience Technology*. "Lessons Learned from Oil Rig Disaster." January 7, 2011. www.biosciencetechnology.com/News/Feeds/2011/01/industries-lessons-learned-from-oil-rig-disaster/.
23. Dyan deNapoli. *The Great Penguin Rescue*. New York: Free Press, 2010, pp. 49–50.
24. deNapoli, *The Great Penguin Rescue*, p. 49.

25. Quoted in PBS. "The Gulf War." *Frontline*, February 4, 1997. www.pbs.org/wgbh/pages/frontline/gulf/script_b.html.

Chapter 3: Environmental Impacts

26. Quoted in Mark Guarino and Peter N. Spotts. "Gulf Oil Spill's Environmental Impact: How Long to Recover?" *Christian Science Monitor*, May 10, 2010. www.csmonitor.com/USA/2010/0510/Gulf-oil-spill-s-environmental-impact-How-long-to-recover.
27. Carolyn Embach. "Oil Spills: Impact on the Ocean." *Water Encyclopedia*. www.waterencyclopedia.com/Oc-Po/Oil-Spills-Impact-on-the-Ocean.html.
28. J.J. Duffy et al. "Oil Spills on Land as Potential Sources of Groundwater Contamination." *Environment International*, vol. 3, 1980, p. 107.
29. Oracle Education Foundation, "Oil Spills."
30. deNapoli, *The Great Penguin Rescue,* p. 3.
31. Quoted in John Keeble. *Out of the Channel: The* Exxon Valdez *Oil Spill in Prince William Sound*. New York: Harper-Collins, 1991, p. 74.
32. Thomas Webler et al. "The Human Dimensions of Oil Spills." Climate Progress, May 5, 2010. http://climateprogress.org/2010/05/05/human-dimensions-bp-oil-spill/.
33. Larry West, "How Do Oil Spills Damage the Environment?" About.com: Environmental Issues. http://environment.about.com/od/petroleum/a/oil_spills_and_environment.htm.

Chapter 4: Economic Impacts

34. Marcus Baram and Gideon Pine. "How the Economic Impact of the Oil Spill Is Spreading Beyond the Gulf." *Huffington Post*, July 15, 2010. www.huffingtonpost.com/2010/07/15/oil-spill-economic-impact_n_646016.html.
35. Ariel Bleicher. "Gulf Power Plants Keep Close Watch on Oil Spill." *IEEE Spectrum*, May 2010. http://spectrum.ieee.org/energy/fossil-fuels/gulf-power-plants-keep-close-watch-on-oil-spill.
36. Mark Schrope. "The Lost Legacy of the Last Great Oil Spill." *Nature* News, July 14, 2010. www.nature.com/news/2010/100714/full/466304a.html.

37. International Tanker Owners Pollution Federation Limited (ITOPF). "Economic Impacts." www.itopf.com/marine-spills/effects/economic-impacts/index.html.

38. Art Davidson. *In the Wake of the* Exxon Valdez: *The Devastating Impact of the Alaska Oil Spill.* San Francisco: Sierra Club Books, 1990, pp. 207–208.

39. Larry West, "Profile: *Exxon Valdez* Oil Spill." About.Com: Environmental Issues. http://environment.about.com/od/environmentalevents/p/exxon_valdez.htm.

40. Allison Linn. "States Fret About Spill's Economic Impact." MSNBC.com. www.msnbc.msn.com/id/36943179/ns/business-us_business.

41. Quoted in Linn, "States Fret About Spill's Economic Impact."

Chapter 5: Cleaning Up Oil Spills

42. William R. Freudenburg and Robert Gramling. *Blowout in the Gulf.* Cambridge, MA: MIT Press, 2011, p. 156.

43. Paul Toscano and Daniel Bukszpan. "17 Ways to Clean Up the Gulf Oil Spill." CNBC.com. www.cnbc.com/id/37593652/17_Ways_To_Clean_Up_The_Gulf_Oil_Spill?slide=4.

44. Mallory Nomack. "Oil Spill Control Technologies." *Encyclopedia of the Earth*, September 8, 2010. www.eoearth.org/articles/view/158385/?topic=50366.

45. Nomack, "Oil Spill Control Technologies."

46. Quoted in Linda R. Sittenfeld. "Chemical-Eating Microbes Might Clean Up Gulf Oil." CNBC.com, June 9, 2010. www.cnbc.com/id/37596590.

47. Sandra Upson. "Oil-Eating Microbes for Gulf Spill." *IEEE Spectrum.* http://spectrum.ieee.org/energy/environment/oileating-microbes-for-gulf-spill.

48. Cameron Scott. "Hyper-Absorbant Peat Moss Could Clean Up Oil Spills Like Louisiana's." Inhabitat, April 30, 2010. http://inhabitat.com/hyper-absorbant-peat-moss-could-clean-up-oil-spills-like-louisianas/.

Chapter 6: Prevention of Oil Spills

49. U.S. Senate Committee on Environment & Public Works. "Oil Pollution Act of 1990." http://epw.senate.gov/opa90.pdf.

50. Alaric Nightingale and Tony Hopfinger. "No Lessons Learned from Exxon Valdez." Center for International Environmental Law, April 16, 2009. www.alphabetics.info/international/?tag=supertankers.

51. Quoted in U.S. Department of Transportation. "U.S. Coast Guard: Statement of Rear Admiral Robert C. North on Double Hull Requirements for Tanker Vessels," June 29, 1999. http://testimony.ost.dot.gov/test/pasttest/99test/North1.htm.

52. Quoted in *Seattle Times*. "Oil Company to Buy Tankers with Double Hulls," April 11, 1990. http://community.seattletimes.nwsource.com/archive/?date=19900411&slug=1065959.

53. Marshall Brain. "A Simple Proposal to Prevent Future Oil Spills: Require Oil Companies to Drill the Relief Wells First." HowStuffWorks, May 26, 2010. http://blogs.howstuffworks.com/2010/05/26/a-simple-proposal-to-prevent-future-oil-spills/.

54. National Oceanic and Atmospheric Administration. "An Oil Spill Primer for Students." http://oceanservice.noaa.gov/education/stories/oilymess/downloads/primer.pdf.

Chapter 1: Why the World Uses So Much Oil

1. List three ways that people in ancient Mesopotamia used bitumen (petroleum), according to Roman scholar Pliny the Elder and Greek historian Herodotus.
2. How did George Bissell's method of obtaining oil from the ground differ from that of the Seneca Indians? Why was his method more effective?
3. Explain how modern industrialized countries allowed themselves to become dependent on oil.

Chapter 2: The Causes of Oil Spills

1. Describe how the large oil seep on the island of Trinidad was found and how it was subsequently exploited.
2. Discuss the ways in which the causes of the *Sansinena* and *Exxon Valdez* disasters differed.
3. What and where was the largest oil release in history? Describe the destructive effects of this event on the environment.

Chapter 3: Environmental Impacts

1. List and explain four possible fates for various fractions of a big oil spill.
2. Describe how the sinking of the ship *Treasure* off South Africa's coast affected the local penguin population. According to American volunteer Jane Stanfield, how were these birds cleaned?
3. What are the dangers to oil cleanup workers? How do these dangers differ from the indirect effects of toxic oil?

Chapter 4: Economic Impacts

1. How do oil spills affect large power stations and desalinization plants?

2. What is the "non-use value" in the aftermath of an oil spill? In the case of the *Exxon Valdez* event, which was larger—the non-use value or the amount that Exxon ended up paying in punitive damages?
3. Allison Linn states that the 2010 BP spill could end up negatively affecting local real estate markets. How does a large oil spill potentially hurt such markets?

Chapter 5: Cleaning Up Oil Spills

1. As stated by William R. Freudenburg and Robert Gramling, what is the principal drawback of oil spill cleanups?
2. Name three kinds of oil skimmers and explain how each one works. What is the chief drawback of using skimmers?
3. Discuss the advantages and disadvantages of using the biological approach to cleaning up oil spills. Why does the biological approach work better on land than in the ocean?

Chapter 6: Prevention of Oil Spills

1. Explain the physical difference between single- and double-hulled tanker ships. What happens in the event that the outer hull of a double-hulled vessel ruptures?
2. What is the prevention strategy mentioned by Marshall Brain? How would it keep a spill from happening?
3. Compare the nuclear and solar alternative energy sources. Which, in your opinion, has fewer potential drawbacks? Tell which of the two you would rather see replace oil in the future and explain why.

ORGANIZATIONS TO CONTACT

American Petroleum Institute (API)
1220 L St. NW
Washington, DC 20005
Phone: (202) 682-8000
Website: www.api.org

A trade organization, the API represents the U.S. oil industry, in conducting research on petroleum and its uses, lobbying on behalf of the industry, and publishing reports, position papers, and information sheets.

Council on Alternative Fuels (CAF)
1225 I St. NW, Ste. 320
Washington, DC 20005
Phone: (202) 898-0711

The CAF is made up of a number of companies that produce synthetic and other alternative fuels or seek to develop synthetic fuel technology. Its monthly publication *Alternate Fuel News* provides up-to-date information on alternative fuels.

Environmental Protection Agency (EPA)
Ariel Rios Building, 1200 Pennsylvania Ave. NW
Washington, DC 20460
Phone: (202) 272-0167
Website: www.epa.gov/

The EPA is an agency of the U.S. government. Its task is to protect the country's environment and to control and eliminate pollution of various kinds. The agency creates and enforces regulations designed to identify and fine polluters and clean up sites that have been polluted. The agency's monthly report is the *EPA Activities Update*.

Friends of the Earth
1025 Vermont Ave. NW, Ste. 300
Washington, DC 20005
Phone: (202) 783-7400
Website: www.foe.org/

Dedicated to protecting Earth from environmental catastrophes, Friends of the Earth also seeks to preserve biological diversity. The group strongly supports constructive and responsible energy policies. In addition to its bimonthly newsletter *Friends of the Earth*, the organization has published the book *Crude Awakening: The Oil Mess in America*.

Union of Concerned Scientists (UCS)
Two Brattle Sq., Cambridge, MA 02238
Phone: (617) 547-5552
Fax: (617) 864-9405
E-mail: ucs@ucsusa.org
Website: www.ucsusa.org

UCS's principal aim is to promote responsible public policy in science- and technology-related areas. Arms control, renewable energy to replace oil dependence, and sustainable agriculture are only a few of the programs that the organization supports. It publishes the twice-yearly magazine *Catalyst*, the quarterly newsletter *Earthwise*, and useful reports, including *Greener SUVs* and *Greenhouse Crisis: The American Response*.

United Nations Environment Programme (UNEP)
PO Box 67578
Nairobi, Kenya 00200
+254 20 7621234
Website: www.unep.org

UNEP encourages sustainable human development through sound environmental practices everywhere. The organization provides information on environmental threats to the sea, environmental assessment, environmental management, and the impacts, management, regulations, and sound environmental technologies related to offshore oil and gas activity.

Worldwatch Institute
1776 Massachusetts Ave. NW
Washington, DC 20036-1904
Phone: (202) 452-1999
Fax: (202) 296-7365
Website: www.worldwatch.org/

Worldwatch performs regular research on, analyzes, and calls attention to major problems affecting the world, among them the use of oil and other forms of energy. The institute publishes the annual *State of the World* and the monthly *World Watch*, as well as periodic papers examining energy-related topics.

FOR MORE INFORMATION

Books

Vincenzo Balzani and Nicola Armaroli. *Energy for a Sustainable World: From the Oil Age to the Sun-Powered Future*. New York: Wiley, 2011. This well-researched, easy-to-read volume discusses present energy sources, including oil, and details several alternative sources, including solar, hydroelectric, wind, nuclear, hydrogen fuel cells, tidal, and others.

Bob Cavnar. *Disaster on the Horizon: High Stakes, High Risks, and the Story Behind the Deepwater Well Blowout*. White River Junction, VT: Chelsea Green, 2010. A comprehensive, well-written account of the worst ocean-based oil spill in history.

Mona Chiang et al. *Oil Spill Disaster*. New York: Scholastic, 2010. Though short and aimed at young students, this volume provides a colorful and up-to-date account of the BP oil spill and other similar large-scale accidents.

Art Davidson. *In the Wake of the* Exxon Valdez: *The Devastating Impact of the Alaska Oil Spill*. San Francisco: Sierra Club Books, 1990. The author, an expert on natural resources, gives a minute-by-minute account of the disaster and tells how Alaskans dealt with its terrible effects.

Dyan deNapoli. *The Great Penguin Rescue*. New York: Free Press, 2010. This engaging volume tells the story of an oil spill off the coast of South Africa in 2000 that endangered tens of thousands of penguins and describes how many of them were saved.

Mervin Fingas. *The Basics of Oil Spill Cleanup*. New York: CRC Press, 2000. This is a well-researched volume that covers all the major cleanup methods used in recent decades.

Mervin Fingas. *Oil Spill Science and Technology*. Oxford, UK: Gulf Professional, 2010. Fingas discusses a wide range of environmental effects caused by oil spills, as well as cleanup methods, all in language aimed at younger readers.

Lauri S. Friedman. *Oil: An Opposing Viewpoints Guide*. Detroit: Greenhaven, 2008. This useful little book, written for junior high readers, contains several short but pointed articles that debate various aspects of big oil in today's world.

William R. Freudenburg and Robert Gramling. *Blowout in the Gulf*. Cambridge, MA: MIT Press, 2011. An excellent, easy-to-read overview of the 2010 BP oil spill and its environmental, economic, and political effects.

David Goodstein. *Out of Gas: The End of the Age of Oil*. New York: Norton, 2004. A frank discussion of humanity's large-scale use of oil and the various alternatives that have been proposed.

August Greeley. *Sludge and Slime: Oil Spills in Our World*. New York: Powerkids, 2003. Aimed at juvenile readers, this is a nicely illustrated, informative book that tells the basics of the subject.

Robert E. Hernon et al. *This Borrowed Earth: Lessons from the Fifteen Worst Environmental Disasters Around the World*. New York: Macmillan, 2010. A handsome volume that looks at a number of disasters that have affected the environment, including one of the most infamous oil spills.

John Keeble. *Out of the Channel: The* Exxon Valdez *Oil Spill in Prince William Sound*. New York: HarperCollins, 1991. One of the best of the many books written about this famous environmental disaster.

Leonardo Maugeri. *The Age of Oil: The Mythology, History, and Future of the World's Most Controversial Resource*. Westport, CT: Praeger, 2006. A very readable and informative presentation of the larger market and political forces behind the large-scale use of oil for energy, from the early twentieth century to the present.

Hal Marcovitz. *Is Offshore Drilling Worth the Risks?* San Diego: ReferencePoint Press, 2010. A well thought-out, easy-to-read discussion of the present offshore drilling industry and the various risks it poses to human society.

Carla Mooney. *Oil Spills and Offshore Drilling*. San Diego: ReferencePoint Press, 2010. This volume, written for students, summarizes the oil spills that have been connected to big oil-drilling rigs in the Gulf of Mexico and elsewhere in the world.

Internet Sources

The Encyclopedia of Earth. "The Ixtoc I Oil Spill," August 26, 2010. www.eoearth.org/articles/view/157319. A useful overview of the second biggest oil spill in the ocean after the 2010 BP spill.

Explore North. "The *Exxon Valdez* Oil Spill Disaster," March 24, 1999. http://explorenorth.com/library/weekly/aa032499 .htm. A brief but informative overview of the famous calamity that struck Alaska in 1989.

Institute for the Analysis of Global Security (IAGS). "Threats to Oil Transport." www.iags.org/oiltransport.html. Tells how various factors, including natural forces and terrorism, can menace the enormous global oil transport industry and thereby cause oil spills.

Laura Moss. "The Thirteen Largest Oil Spills in History." Mother Nature Network, July 16, 2010. www.mnn.com/earth-matters/ wilderness-resources/stories/the-13-largest-oil-spills-in-history. This highly informative list is followed by several links to other topics relating to oil and oil spills.

Mother Nature Network. "Huge Oil Spill Cleanup in Kuwait." January 17, 2011. www.mnn.com/earth-matters/wilderness-resources/stories/kuwait-to-clean-up-oil-contamination-from-1990-invasion. Tells how the Iraqis purposely caused a massive oil spill in 1990 and announces that a major cleanup program is planned.

Technology Review. "How to Prevent Deep Water Spills," June 10, 2010. www.technologyreview.com/energy/25525/?a=f. This site, maintained by MIT scientists, offers an alternate, safer design for deep-sea wellheads like the one that broke in the 2010 BP accident in the Gulf of Mexico.

Larry West. "Oil Spills and the Environment." About.com: Environmental Issues. http://environment.about.com/od/pet roleum/a/oil_spills_and_environment.htm. A lively discussion of the ways that oil spills affect the environment, written by noted journalist and science writer Larry West.

INDEX

Piper Alpha oil spill (1979), 37–38
Pliny the Elder, 15, 16
Polar Endeavor (oil tanker), 87
Polo, Marco, 17
Prevention
  improved tanker designs, 86–88
  stricter environmental laws, 84–86
  through decreased dependency on oil, 91–94
Purchasing decisions, to reduce oil use, 92

R
Relief wells, 90–91
Rockefeller, John D., Sr., 21

S
Sansinena explosion (1976), 32–34
Santa Barbara oil spill (1969), 29, 84
Sea Empress spill (Wales, 1996), 79
Shetland Islands oil spill (1993), 10
Skimmers/skimming, 74–75, 75
Social and Environmental Research Institute, 53
Solar power, 91, 93
Sorbents, 76, 78, 79
Southern African Foundation
for the Conservation of Coastal Birds (SANCCOB), 48, 51
Standard Oil Company, 21, 22
Stanfield, Jane, 48

T
Tankers
  improved designs for, 86–88
  registry of, 39–40
Thorpe, Nick, 17
Torrey Canyon oil spill (1967), 35, 37
Transportation, percentage fueled by oil, 25
Treasure oil spill (South Africa, 2000), 49, 51, 52
Trinidad oil pit (Asphalt Lake), 31

U
United States, first oil well in, 20
University of New Hampshire, 9
Upson, Sandra, 82
U.S. Travel Association, 63

W
Wind power, 93
Wobblier, Thomas, 53

X
X Prize Foundation, 83

PICTURE CREDITS

ABOUT THE AUTHOR

In addition to his acclaimed volumes on ancient civilizations, historian Don Nardo has published several books examining important modern discoveries and issues relating to technology and science. These include *Cloning, Lasers, Vaccines, Atoms, Forces and Motion, Space Travel,* and *The Scientific Revolution.* Nardo lives with his wife, Christine, in Massachusetts.